EVERYTH
STARTED AS
NOTHING

Praise for the book

This book gives real insights on what it takes to build a business in the post-Covid era. It comes at a time when large businesses and economies are facing unprecedented challenges while startups are able to adapt much faster. They are re-imagining innovation and business and are showing us the future. The digital revolution has arrived with a bang and the world has suddenly changed. Those who do not change will be history soon!

—**T.V. Mohandas Pai**,
Chairman, Aarin Capital Partners

Bhaskar's insights are razor sharp, particularly when it comes to tech companies and start-ups. As technology takes over more and more industries in India, disruptive start-ups in India have to be taken very seriously, especially by the incumbent players. If you want to understand how to build and scale start-ups in a new emerging ecosystem of India then you need to read this book.

—**Paul Cuatrecasas,**
Founder of Aquaa Partners and author of *GO Tech or GO Extinct*

EVERYTHING STARTED AS NOTHING

HOW TO WIN THE START-UP BATTLE

BHASKAR MAJUMDAR

RUPA

Published by
Rupa Publications India Pvt. Ltd 2021
7/16, Ansari Road, Daryaganj
New Delhi 110002

Sales Centres:
Allahabad Bengaluru Chennai
Hyderabad Jaipur Kathmandu
Kolkata Mumbai

ISBN: 978-93-90547-87-6

Second impression 2021

10 9 8 7 6 5 4 3 2

Printed at Thomson Press India Ltd., Faridabad

The moral right of the author has been asserted.

To my parents, Juthika Majumdar and Dr R.S. Majumdar,
my wife Ratun Lahiri
and
To the entrepreneurial spirit of India that awes and
inspires me with its audacity and ambition.

CONTENTS

FOREWORD

I returned to India in 1999 with the intention to start something of my own. These were the heady days of the dotcom boom and the internet was buzzing with activity.

I always wanted to be in India and was deeply passionate about solving issues here. I have worked in both product and services, and probably got lucky as I sold some ventures. The story of my life has been that: technology has to be the key disruptor of anything you want to do.

This was precisely my thought when I launched ApnaCard in 2000. ApnaCard was a virtual web card that worked just like an actual bank card. But, India's internet population at the time was just about 500,000 and a small fraction made transactions with credit cards. We, of course, had to pivot from being a consumer-centric business to providing technology services to businesses, and ended up having more than 100 clients.

As a tech entrepreneur, I think India missed the dotcom boom that had happened globally and the bust from 1998 to 2000. India was just not ready. In the year 2000, the number of internet users in India was miniscule—this also meant that our digital payments system was poor.

THE START-UP ECOSYSTEM

I always remember what my father said when I started my entrepreneurial journey: 'If you can drive a car in Delhi, you can drive anywhere.' What this meant was, the kind of problems you have to solve to get a start-up up and running in India is extraordinary.

Though we missed the bus in 2000, the next wave came in 2010–11 when a lot of NRIs started returning to India, including some who had tasted success with their ventures in the US. So, some of the unicorns you see now are a result of that period. Parallel to this, the Indian internet segment also started to pick-up. We were still missing many pieces of the puzzle, like we still didn't have e-KYC, our delivery and banking systems were broken and there were several entry barriers.

The era of 2010–11 also produced the first level of entrepreneurs in e-commerce, payment and shared economy. These start-ups were truly outside the comfort zone and still made it big.

The paradigm shift in the Indian entrepreneurial eco-system happened with the merging of Digital India and Start-up India (2014–15). I am a firm believer that India, now, is not only looking to innovate for itself, but for the next six billion people of this planet. That is the audacious goal we have. At the end of the day, there are nine platforms in the world which have a billion users. Five are from Silicon Valley, four from China and the tenth platform is the India Stack. These nine platforms solve the problems of one billion people—there are six billion more whose needs have to be catered to, and I think Indian start-ups can do that not only for India but for similar countries.

Today's shift in the start-up eco-system in India is not because of the 'me-too' kind of start-ups. The shift is happening because of start-ups that are solving tough problems. They are local to India. There is also a realization that the Indian start-up is bit-sized in nature, as the Indian consumer is a sachet consumer. Volumes are high but the value per transaction can be low.

In areas like education, finance and healthcare, Indian start-ups have led the way. What we are doing in these segments is unlike anywhere else in the world. I think our start-ups are the best. For instance, during the COVID pandemic, Indian start-ups were becoming contactless as fast as those in any other country. Telemedicine platforms were being offered within 15 days. When some of the overseas data harvesting apps were banned overnight, we had multiple start-ups that provided better alternatives.

The government initiative Digital India AatmaNirbhar Bharat Innovate Challenge has 7,000 applicants in 10 different categories. One can just imagine the scale of innovation happening in India. At present, there are more than 50,000 registered start-ups, but there are more than double that number of unregistered start-ups.

From a mindset point, we as an innovating start-up community have started to make a dent. In 2005–06, people wanted to work in big companies. They would explain, 'If I do not work for a big company, my prospects of marriage are very bleak.' Today, people retort, 'If you are so smart, then why aren't you doing something on your own.' There is a clear shift in the mindset. When this change happens at the level of college education, you see innovation.

The next buzzwords for the entrepreneurial eco-system in India are Artificial Intelligence and deep tech like blockchain. From being a data-poor country, we have developed into a data-rich country, with a diversity of data that needs to be harnessed. Going ahead, the role of our research community will be significant to create businesses out of this data.

When the present lot of entrepreneurs are compared to those from two decades ago, there is a marked increase in both quality and confidence in the entrepreneurs. The Indian entrepreneur has realized the value of understanding the domestic market. They know they will have an advantage if they operate in India and understand the consumer well. That is their advantage over a global company coming to India and trying to start something.

When these entrepreneurs take on the big daddies from the US, they know they can compete because they understand the market well. This has completely changed from a couple of years ago, when entrepreneurs would not venture into a segment if they knew there was a global player in it. Today even if there is a GooglePay, there are five other players who claim they can also do what GooglePay does, and do it better.

DIGITAL INDIA

The Indian entrepreneurial story got a push from the Digital India (DI) roadmap that the government laid out in 2014. The vision of DI is that the use of technology at speed and scale will rapidly increase the reach of education, content and services, to solve problems.

The DI programme has roots in the vision that Prime Minister

Narendra Modi had laid out in mid-June 2014. He had said that while cities in the past were built on riverbanks, they are now built along highways. But in the future, they would be built based on the availability of optical fiber networks and next-generation infrastructure.

DI's vision is to empower a billion Indians who are living in villages across the country and speak their native language. This is being done by bringing together three fundamental frameworks:

1. Digital infrastructure, high speed data connectivity and easy access to affordable devices and data.
2. A software foundation with biometrics-based Aadhaar services as the basis, and add-ons like mobile payment gateways, e-KYC via digital payments lockers and secured cloud lockers. This is the basic India Stack available to everyone.
3. Destinations like e-governance, tax administration, direct benefit transfers and the creation of the start-up eco-system.

The DI map it is about the hardware foundation, software foundation and, to top it up, destinations like e-governance, payments and the start-up ecosystem. This has kick-started a major disruption.

Let us look at what the DI initiative has managed to achieve so far:

1. India today has the lowest cost of data per GB/month.
2. Data consumption in India has gone up by 55 times in the last five years, and cost has gone down by 42 times.
3. Internet connectivity has gone up from 150 million to 700 million.
4. The last 100 million users have come from non-urban areas.

This technological revolution also belongs to Bharat, with 70 per cent of the country's population residing in villages, which is an equal stakeholder and beneficiary of the digital revolution. At present, 155,739 gram panchayats have laid down optical fiber and this number is to touch 2.5 lakh. Under the Common Services Centres (CSCs) 2.0 scheme, over 370,000 lakh centres across the country have processed 10 crore crop insurance applications, made 269,000 Ayushman Bharat cards, registered 30,55,000 workers for the unorganized sector pension scheme and on-boarded 10.84 lakh Wi-Fi users.

In the last six years, since the launch of the DI, about 1.25 billion Indians have the Aadhaar identity system available to them. The UPI framework in FY20 clocked 12.5 billion transaction worth ₹21.31 trillion, and the digital locker has become the go-to app for digital issuance and verification of certificates and documents. Since its inception in 2015, the DigiLocker has digitized over 430 million insurance policies and the Income Tax Department has provided PAN verification records to over 365 million citizens. The amalgamation of the Aadhaar and software layer of India Stack allowed the creation of over 350 million Jan Dhan accounts.

Jan Dhan, Aadhaar and DI have started a disruption in the banking and payment industry, the success and uptake of which has been appreciated and adopted by global technology giants like Google and WhatsApp. This shows India is no longer simply following the innovation of others.

The Goods and Services Tax (GST) was the first step towards ease of doing business for the micro, small and medium enterprises (MSME) segment. In just one move, 17 national and state taxes that had been impeding trade and business in the country, were replaced by a single nationwide tax. While the initial deployment of the GST was hampered by excessive complexity and other challenges of execution, the uptake of the new system has nonetheless been rapid and widespread. As of now, 1.26 crore taxpayers have registered on the GST website. GST has amplified a seamless and hassle-free taxation process in the country.

If I have to do some crystal gazing, it is my opinion that the future will see major breakthrough and innovation in the access to credit for the Indian masses.

Under the DI umbrella, policy enablement also gives value to the data output layer, which is the cause for the Personal Data Protection (PDP) bill coming up. India is one of the only countries that recognizes the need for a balance among innovation, regulation and privacy.

For instance, with the PDP bill becoming law, the micro-credit and credit facilities that have been mentioned so far, like credit on the fly and credit for all, will become a reality. From the MSME perspective, be it a small manufacturer or a Kirana shop, the whole gamut of services around inventory management, analytics, reducing their working capital, knowing their customers better, etc. will ease up.

As a technology entrepreneur, I feel that policy makers need to keep up the pace. While regulation does become an enabler, it also does not keep track of technology. Regulation lags technology, and hence innovation does happen in a grey area. I feel that the forward-looking policies in India should be enabling in their nature.

In India, even in the fast-track mode, a bill easily takes a year's time to become a policy. With a one-year long process and with Moore's law applicable to technology, you never know if what you started now will be able to hold its direction. This is not good for entrepreneurs as their window for innovation gets crunched. So, keeping this in mind, having a policy that is enabling and overarching is better than being prescriptive. I also foresee an increase in self-regulation coming into India—various small regulators within industries, who will have a set of regulations for their players to adhere to.

TECHNOLOGY FOR POLITICAL CHANGE

I believe that technology can disrupt our democratic process too, in the right way. I think we can use technology to engage with people in our political system and use it to bring positive change. This was the reason why I pivoted from technology to politics in 2009.

Today, I am glad that every political party and process in this country is talking about digital platforms that can be used for citizen engagement. I was laughed at in 2010, but then that's what disruption is all about; when you start, you start small, and then with the success, you move on.

In the years from 2010–15, it was all about showcasing how technology can bring about big changes. They were both internal and external disbelievers. I joined the Bharatiya Janata Party (BJP) to solve this problem and I felt the leadership in BJP was much more open to do this; they accepted an outsider to come in and bring about these changes. Today, this transformation in the political realm is a case study globally.

One of the biggest challenges for me as a social and political entrepreneur has been mindset change. But the job of an entrepreneur is to make way through all the challenges. In my professional journey, I have been a tech entrepreneur, and a political entrepreneur who created a start-up within a political party, funded it with our own resources, generated funds to support the small team we had, and we were net cash positive outfit within the party.

We set up India's first online donation platform. I still remember ICICI Bank's response when I called them to set up an online account. They asked what BJP was and 'which e-commerce player/product are you?' They said nobody has ever asked for this. Ten years ago, this was unheard of.

Running an outfit as a CEO in a government organization (Mygov.in) taught me so much about making things run within the given framework, while still getting outputs. The lessons I learnt as a tech, social and political entrepreneur have been diverse and enriching. I think, at the end of the day, you must solve problems as an entrepreneur.

The influence of technology in politics is now maturing. Data and digital platforms will play a key role as we move forward, and will be beneficial for a democratic society. Technology is lot more transparent, visible and accountable. Smart principles are increasingly being applied to tech. In politics, the whole approach should not be to use tech to merely run campaigns, but to use it to solve problems and create an engagement process.

As an entrepreneur involved in both business and politics, I believe in creating small victories, creating a mindset shift, creating ambassadors who will believe in you. We need to think of high speed and scale, otherwise we won't make a mark in either business or society.

One needs to re-imagine change.

Arvind Gupta
1 December 2020

(Arvind Gupta is a technology entrepreneur who built a product and services firm and exited the same. He has been a corporate leader having worked with global multi-national companies and has also donned the avatar of an investor for a short while, and managed to get some good exits. He has been a social and political entrepreneur. He created a start-up within the country's largest political party, the Bharatiya Janata Party, and was CEO

xvi   BHASKAR MAJUMDAR

of a government initiative, running it like a start-up. Arvind Gupta has worn almost all the hats that an entrepreneur can wish to wear. He is also an Eisenhower Fellow for Innovation).

INTRODUCTION

It was in mid-2019 that I finally managed to get to speak to Abhishek Negi, who recently founded Eggoz. In his previous avatar, he was co-founder of cab aggregator Roder, which Unicorn India Ventures, an early-stage technology-focused venture fund co-founded by Anil Joshi and me, had invested in. I had been trying to get in touch with Abhishek for over a year but had been unable to do so. When I asked him about his sudden disappearance, his response baffled me. He said, 'How could I show you my face after the failure of my business. You had invested in it with such faith in me.'

Roder shut down its operations in 2017, as competition from well-entrenched players like Ola and Uber in the intra-city segment had made it difficult for a start-up to survive. Once the business winded up, Abhishek vanished from the face of this earth. He just became incommunicado.

As an investor in over 30 businesses across India and UK, with aggregated valuation of well over $2 billion dollars, and as an entrepreneur having exited three businesses, I understand that businesses survive and they fail but what does not and should not fail is the entrepreneurial spirit. When I heard Abhishek that day, I felt that a business had failed, not an entrepreneur. It immediately got me reminiscing my journey and within that journey, the encounters I have had with CEOs, investors, management gurus and entrepreneurs et al. It brought back all the discussions I have had with each of them and how they dealt with success and failure. By the end of the day, I had decided to write a book for the entrepreneurs in the Indian context. Books that are available tend to be either those written by Western authors or those built around the success of an entrepreneur. There's no book that looks at the entire Indian entrepreneurial start-up ecosystem and analyses the different types of businesses that have either succeeded of failed.

A book which provides a comprehensive 'what works and what doesn't' in the Indian context, with anecdotes and real-life stories of entrepreneurial success and failure, across technology, agri- and small-scale businesses, spanning manufacturing and social sectors, will have a mass appeal and cut right across the length and breadth of the country.

You may wonder, why specifically the Indian context? India is not new to entrepreneurial zeal and stories but despite all that, we, as a culture and society, do not encourage entrepreneurship and look down on failure, which is an intrinsic part of an entrepreneur's journey. Even today, when we have emerged as the third largest country of entrepreneurs, parents want children to immediately take up a well-paying job.

One of the other reasons why people often curbed their inner drive of starting a business is because there was no framework of scalable entrepreneurship in India, till the last two decades. For entrepreneurs to be able to scale up, they need access to funding, equal market opportunity, support from the government and a supportive societal framework.

The MSME sector has played a crucial role in the creation of employment and revenue in India. Today, the MSME sector in India contributes 29.7 per cent to the GDP[1] and about 45 per cent to the overall exports of the country, but look closely and you will see their struggle. This is what I meant when I said there is a need for a framework of scalable entrepreneurship, which is now being created in India.

◆

One of the other reasons for writing this book was the general perception people have of start-ups. Nowadays, start-ups get highlighted for the wrong reasons. Chronicling an entrepreneur's journey for others to understand is always worthy, but to make founders feel like demi-gods, especially in a place like India, because they managed to raise funds, and to splash their

---

[1]'MSMEs Contribute 29.7% Of India's GDP'. *Business Standard*, www.business-standard. com/article/news-cm/msmes-contribute-29-7-of-india-s-gdp-119120200888_1.html. Accessed 21 November 2020.

images across media creates unnecessary pressure within the eco-system. If getting a story and picture published in media (newspaper/magazines/online portals) becomes a benchmark for founders, it will indeed belittle the efforts of starting a business.

Starting on your own is a tough choice and the road is full of hurdles; instead of concentrating on the business roadmap, if the founder gets hassled because his start-up has not been written about, then they are taking on unnecessary pressure. The need for attention is an Indian phenomenon. In the Valley, technology businesses are built in the stealth mode for a long time and they surface once they are ready for primetime.

I had started my entrepreneurial journey 20 years ago, in 2000. Since then, a lot has changed—India has changed—and yet the factors that are key for an entrepreneur to succeed have not changed and might never in the future.

As an entrepreneur, I understand the challenges of building a business from ground up. As a former entrepreneur, I connect with the founders, understand their apprehensions and am able to suggest options to grow their businesses because I have been through the same cycle of excitement, anxiety, fear and success.

◆

Entrepreneurship is a state of mind. It isn't merely about implementation of an idea. It is about risk taking, putting your head above the parapet and trying to create something out of nothing. One may be successful as a corporate executive, student or research fellow, but that does not necessarily mean that one has the entrepreneurial DNA.

I am often asked if there is a right time to start a venture, or to leave a job to take the plunge into an entrepreneurial journey. Frankly, there is no straight answer. As an entrepreneur, I can only say that one should follow their 'gut'. It is an intuitive feeling. And when one is ready, one just knows it. I also believe that entrepreneurs are those who will roll with the punches and find opportunities. Though all this is true, it is crucial to always keep your ears to the ground to know if an opportunity is one that will have demand in the long run.

The other most asked question is about the right age. Again, there is no straight answer for this. Starting early has its pros and cons, and those who venture into start-ups in their 40s too have faced repercussions. The only thing an entrepreneur should do is believe in their idea and not treat it as a stop gap arrangement, so that when things do not move well, they can get onto another job.

In my case, my first venture Recreate Solutions, was started as an opportunity I spotted as digitization started to take the centerstage among enterprises. Since I was working with a media firm, AltaVista, I could clearly see that there was a need for such a service and a cross-border business provided the perfect platform for this, given India had always excelled at any process transition.

This book has stories of why some people continued to be serial entrepreneurs and go through the twists and turns of the entrepreneurial ride, rather than take up a well-paying corporate job.

◆

One of the criteria for selecting people for this book was to find the quintessential Indian story. Their ideas have to be the solutions that India is looking for. I also did not want to restrict myself to the tech-industry, though it is a fact that technology has become all-pervasive, and now has become the backbone of every business, irrespective of sector.

It was a tough choice to select the people I wanted to feature in the book. In the last three decades of my life, spanning from my educational and professional stints across three countries, I have had the good fortune of knowing people who have managed to create a niche for themselves, as well as, become icons for their generation. I am thankful to Arvind Gupta for penning down his thoughts on the overall Indian start-up landscape and for detailing how Indian businesses are distinct from those of the West. He also speaks of the 'India model' being replicated in new frontier markets.

The book has a mix of young digital entrepreneurs who are ambitious and have raised substantial venture capital, and are driving the 'Digital India' story. Within these pages are the stories of Amod Malviya (the young founder of India's fastest unicorn Udaan), Abhinay Choudhari (a quintessential entrepreneur who didn't let failures deter him and went on to co-found BigBasket) and Phanindra Sama (the quiet and humble founder of India's first consumer business exit, Redbus).

Also featured are seasoned IT entrepreneurs who have run their businesses organically for decades without substantial funding, like Rajat Mohanty, who built a cyber security company Paladion, for two decades and sold it to Atos Origin, and Anand Deshpande, who ventured into the product development management space when the IT industry was obsessed with services and transformed Persistent Systems into a successful IPO.

In addition to the technology arena, the book draws on the learning of entrepreneurs from different industries, like the hospitality industry. Anjan Chaterjee, the founder of Speciality Restaurants (Oh! Calcutta and Mainland China) has seen the restaurant business grow over the last 25 years, and was the first to taste IPO success in this industry. Celebrity chef and businessman Sanjeev Kapoor single-handedly brought chefs out of the closet and made them stars in India. In sports, entrepreneur Saumil Majmudar created a business out of his passion.

When we hear about entrepreneurship, we think of the hard-nosed world of business. But the realm of entrepreneurship cuts across fields. I have been fortunate to speak to Venkat Krishnan, my ex-colleague who gave up his successful corporate career to build GiveIndia, which became India's foremost platform for philanthropic donations and scaled it further to create Daan Utsav. His passion for scale, building teams and strategic vision made GiveIndia a scalable social enterprise.

I was fortunate to get my friend Rajesh Jain (India's first internet entrepreneur and who created and exited IndiaWorld) to share his entrepreneurial experiences. The versatile Sanjay Anandaram has shared his thoughts on entrepreneurship in the political and social arena for this book.

The book draws upon the experiences of senior corporate executives who have transformed themselves and created large start-up businesses. I have featured Sudip Bandyopadhyay, who after a stellar corporate career in large enterprises launched his own 'listed start-up'. Other senior corporate executives too have elaborated on the challenges they faced as they entered the road to entrepreneurship. This transition is not easy and I had struggled to cope with this change in my first venture Recreate Solutions, as I had embarked on a start-up after leaving a senior position in a global media business. It is, indeed, interesting to hear their stories.

As companies grow, they induct senior professionals, who though not 'founders' need to have a similar DNA to be able to scale up these businesses. They often outshine the founders and the interplay of relationship between them and the founders is remarkably interesting to watch. Phaneesh Murthy, who built the sales engine of Infosys and was the driver for the growth phase of the business, speaks openly on the challenges of senior executives as they come into the start-up world and also, on what is needed to take a company from the start-up phase to the consolidation phase.

◆

It was in 2015 that I decided to become an institutional investor. Prior to that, I was investing my own capital both in India as well as the UK, but it had its limitations. The biggest limitation is the inability to scale your investments. Being a single investor with my own funds, I could invest in very few companies. This meant higher risks as well as higher returns. At the same time, the early-stage investment scene was starting to gain momentum in India and globally.

The real drive for me to get into early-stage institutional investment was the fact that I was placing my bet on an entrepreneur or start-up, early in their lifecycle. The other drive was the fact that I could bring my learning as an entrepreneur and investor to the table, for a portfolio of companies.

At Unicorn India Ventures, our philosophy is business first, funding later. Thus, my partner Anil Joshi and I spend a long time with entrepreneurs who come to us for funding. We and the team take 3–4 months to understand their business model, the team at work, revenue streams, etc. This mentoring is provided to them without any mention of signing a cheque. In many cases, we tell entrepreneurs to tap into new revenue streams which may have been in their blind spot or which they may be aware of, but don't know how to approach. Only after spending considerable time with businesses, do we discuss funding them.

We want Unicorn to be a different player in India's early-stage investment eco-system. With Unicorn, we have aimed to do things differently in every sphere; whether it's about adopting a different strategy of evaluating start-ups or reaching out investors.

◆

Everything Started as Nothing has been written by me as an investor and I have tried to include all those scenarios that a start-up has to undergo as it treads along its course.

I sometimes feel that entrepreneurship and the need to be successful has made us forget that all large companies and booming Unicorns had humble beginnings—it's not too far-fetched to say that they all started with nothing. Just like zero comes before one, your success, or failure even, is based on moving from zero to one and on and on.

When we read stories of successful businesses or individuals, we tend to focus on and remember them for their billions of dollars of revenue or uniqueness, but we tend to forget or neglect how they started. Everyone started from the bottom—a garage, a dorm room or a small flat.

I have written this book with four stages of an entrepreneurial journey in mind—the infancy stage, the growth stage, the consolidation stage and the end game. Each section will draw out the challenges that a start-up founder faces at each stage of the journey. The headwinds at each stage of growth are very different. Each stage needs a different mindset and attributes to overcome the adversity. The sections will bring out that facet, as often, the entrepreneur who is great in starting up faces insurmountable difficulties as the business grows.

During the **infancy stage**, I have tried to capture the early days of the founder. This would typically be the first couple of years since the idea germinated in the mind of the entrepreneur. I have attempted to showcase the determination that one needs before one embarks on this journey. For every success, there are countless failures and even a successful entrepreneur has been to the brink a couple of times in his journey.

The book deals with questions such as, what goes on in the mind of the entrepreneur before they finally take the plunge? When is the right time to start? What is the right balance between entrepreneurs who say 'let us just go ahead and we'll see' and those entrepreneurs who are 'caught in their own tangle of analysis and paralysis'?

Every start-up is fraught with risks. I have tried to throw some light on how an entrepreneur can plan his business. What is the business that he is in? How can he use historical 'analogs' and 'antilogs' to determine the potential of business success?

The role of co-founders in a start-up is extremely important as the entrepreneurship journey is a lonely one. And founders need co-founders to be by their side during the tough times of starting and scaling up a business. What is the skillset your co-founder needs to have? This co-founder dynamic can often make or break a fledgling start-up.

The key to success in the infancy stage is to take calculated risks, explore new ideas, tweak your business model based on market feedback, formalize processes that have proven to work and be able to bring outside investment into the business. This is the critical juncture in many entrepreneurs' careers, since the start-up phase is where most businesses fail. Crossing this stage to the next does not rule that you are out of the woods but does increase your chance of survival.

The **growth stage** begins once you have raised the initial seed funding, developed the Minimum Viable Product (MVP), figured out the initial business model and initial customer base. Quite a few companies fail to reach this stage. The growth stage transforms a 'start-up' to a 'scale-up'.

How one performs in this phase determines if the start-up will be able to become an enterprise. To successfully make it through the growth stage, you need to hunker down and formalize all of your workflows and operating systems. As your team expands and you make critical hires, one of the keys to business growth is to have standard processes that all team members can easily follow. You need to raise constant capital and be able to ensure the right spend for the growth.

The **consolidation stage** is an interesting time for the founder. This is the phase where the organization becomes larger than the founder. Their idea has finally morphed into an enterprise. Most companies which reach this phase have raised considerable amounts of funding across multiple rounds. The consolidation stage is more about the organization than the entrepreneur. This is the first time where there is a divergence of the two.

The book also chronicles the journey of the entrepreneur after he becomes delinked from the company. In the last section, the **end game**, I have dealt with issues like life after the business has matured and is ready to function on its own. What's next for the founders? The entrepreneurs have also elaborated on the timing of an exit.

◆

I have enjoyed every step of this process of writing this book. I have made the most of re-connecting with old friends and getting to know some new entrepreneurs for this book. I thank each and every one of them to have believed in my pursuit and for giving me their precious time. I hope you enjoy reading it just as much.

1

START-UP SUCCESS STORIES ARE GLAMORIZED, BE READY FOR THE GRIND AND GRIME

Every week, Unicorn Ventures India, the fund I started, gets over 300 business plans from students, youngsters and seasoned professionals across various domains. For a country with a population of 1.3 billion, this number is perhaps justifiable. But entrepreneurship is a leap of faith, and though my team and I are always looking for a good idea, I am constantly trying to gauge the intent of the person in setting up their business.

As an entrepreneur, before I had started the fund, I experienced the whole gamut of the entrepreneurial journey. And trust me when I say it is not a walk in the park. It may look glamorous, given the way many of the stories that we see are depicted in the media, but that is far from the truth. Open any business newspaper and magazine, and success stories of start-ups are aplenty. Platforms such as Forbes's '30 under 30' and Fortune's '40 Under 40' provide instant gratification to entrepreneurs, satiating their ego.

Such platforms do matter, as they help motivate and celebrate all the risk and hard work undertaken by an entrepreneur. But this media hype in recent years has added a 'glamour quotient' to start-ups; this perceived 'coolness' associated with start-ups has inspired many students and young executives to become entrepreneurs. In reality, the start-up journey is fraught with difficulties and can get very lonely. Irrespective of the type of start-up and the age of the entrepreneur, all start-up founders need to be aware of some of the challenges they will face as they begin their journey.

I give credit to my wife Ratun for my entrepreneurial journey. She is a quintessential big company professional, having worked at large enterprises across various geographies, but she understood my dreams and was there by my side through thick and thin. In fact, when you feel lonely and desolate, you need your close ones to pull you out of the mental morass.

Even when India has woken up to the potential of entrepreneurship, Indian parents remain hesitant when told that their child wants to establish their own business. The pressure of being an unknown and not being under the protective umbrella of a company or government job amplifies the parental pressure already on the young founder. As the entrepreneur embarks on their journey, it is important that they have their family's support—be it their spouse or parents.

For an entrepreneur, there is no clear demarcation between home and office, and the highs and lows of the journey are felt by the entire family. Having familial support is therefore, crucial and that is why early-stage investors spend a lot of time trying to gauge the family aspect of an entrepreneur and their risk-taking and sustainability potential.

Pankit Desai, co-founder of Sequretek, who started his cybersecurity business after a successful corporate career in his mid-40s says, 'I clearly remember the day when I broke this news to my family. They threw a fit. And I was faced with a volley of questions, starting from why at this age, to what if I fail, to financial support and security issues.'

Pankit also shared that starting in the 40s is filled with challenges, many of which do not exist when you are in your 30s or 50s. 'When we started, I was 43 and my children were yet to start on their higher educational journey and I was adamant that their education would not be compromised because of my entrepreneurial stint. But if you look closely , there are financial aspects that come with this age, which is not so much if you are in your 30s or 50s. For those who start in their 40s, failing also has its challenges. In case things do not go as planned, then returning to a corporate life at 50 is not a comfortable proposition.'

Pankit further adds, 'Backing of the family is particularly important and without that, one cannot even think of succeeding. For instance, we moved from a rented four-bedroom apartment facing the Lake at Powai to Goregaon. I had to think about reducing costs.'

Any person who wants to start on his own needs to be mentally prepared to move away from their regular lifestyle and for that, the unstinted support of the entire family is essential. The pressures of a start-up will always be there, and one can't afford extraneous pressures from any other quarters specially the family.

VAGARIES OF A START-UP RIDE

We all have heard of the intelligence quotient, emotional quotient and social quotient but the make and break quotient for an entrepreneur is the 'adversity quotient'. This is the measure of the ability to go through a rough patch without losing one's bearings. For an early-stage founder, everyday adversity stares them in the face, and they need to be able to take it on the chin.

The common belief is that entrepreneurs exhibit a streak of narcissism, craziness and infectious optimism. But what is not well known is that successful founders need to have a tough mind to go through the ups and down of this ride. Often, passionate people tend to be emotional but not so in the case of entrepreneurs. While passion drives an entrepreneur, they cannot be emotional. The life of an early-stage founder is akin to a roller coaster ride. On some days, rejections can be rife, making them suffer from a crisis of confidence which toggles alongside the emotional highs, bordering on arrogance, when things go right.

The strangest thing is that in the life of a start-up, the highs and lows can be experienced by the founder within a matter of hours. From euphoria to thinking the world is falling apart and back to euphoria, are all part of the daily cycle of an entrepreneur. A good call with a client who might buy your hitherto untested product can send you into an emotional high, only to be shattered within minutes as you hear a rejection, with no reason cited, from an investor whose funding was vital to be able to complete the product.

These highs and lows can be difficult to handle and it is no secret that many start-up founders suffer from mental illness, which in some cases has also led to entrepreneurs committing suicide. The untimely death of V.G. Siddhartha, founder of Café Coffee Day, highlights the pressure that entrepreneurs go through. As one wishes to embark on the journey of entrepreneurship, one needs to be aware of these underbellies of entrepreneurship which are not discussed openly.

Azim Premji, founder of Wipro, had rightly pointed out that equanimity is the single most important attribute of a founder.

NO LOOKING BACK

One of the challenges I grappled with when I started my first start-up Recreate Solutions in 2000 was the sheer anonymity of being a start-up founder. I had been at a senior global leadership position in a global media behemoth and had enjoyed the trappings of the corporate world. When I started my first venture, I was suddenly bereft of the corporate 'calling card'.

In every discussion, I would be on the defensive and try to draw on the credibility of my past corporate career. I would fumble when asked what I was doing now and would always qualify the answer by saying it was a venture-backed start-up and how many people there were in the company.

The people asking these questions and my colleagues could have certainly perceived my discomfort in my answers. This was a manifestation of my inherent insecurity. It took me around two years to grow out of this mindset and once I made peace with myself, there was no looking back.

This is more relevant to executives-turned-entrepreneurs, but it also stands true for young start-up founders. Their academic peers, working for large companies, would draw a good pay-cheque and an identity from their employers, while the new entrepreneur on the block would be a 'nobody' and their start-up identity will be of no relevance to anyone.

Sudip Bandyopadhyay, Group Chairman, Inditrade always regales me with stories of his early days as an entrepreneur. He had had a stellar corporate career with Hindustan Unilever, ITC, Reliance and private equity firm New Silk Route before he embarked on his entrepreneurial journey to start Inditrade, a digitally driven non-banking financial corporation (NBFC). Says Sudip, 'As it happens when you are holding a CXO position in a big corporate, people make a beeline to be in your office, but when I started Inditrade, no bank was ready to immediately come on board and back us. These were the same guys who would be after me at ITC where I used to head the Treasury & Investments. At Reliance, I also had a huge operation and would be chased by all financiers. With Inditrade, though an established company and one that came through an acquisition, I had to create the basic infrastructure and trust among business constituents afresh, and it was clearly a learning for me. In hindsight, I realize that people were seeing if I could pull this off, but at that point it was painful to endure.'

Peter Thiel has aptly remarked in *Zero to One*: 'Entrepreneurship has no optionality.' It is a one-way street. You must burn the bridge of return, else you will look to the escape route whenever you hit a speed bump. Remember, to succeed as an entrepreneur, you must not look at the start-up as an option and always be ready with a plan B. 'I will try my hand at start-up,' is never the right approach.

Rajat Mohanty, who built a business for over 20 years in the cyber security services segment, Paladion, and eventually sold to Atos, articulates this, 'I think many founders pack off early. At Paladion, we went through extreme rough patches, but we had the strength to go on despite the pain. Entrepreneurial success is all about enduring the pain and having the perseverance.' It is always easy to look at successful companies in awe, but we must remember that everything starts with nothing. If you are one of those who looks at large companies and feels as though you can never achieve something that grand, then you can't. Rajat knew that there were large players in the cyber security segment, but that didn't dampen his resolve; instead, he focused on taking it one step at a time and reached his goal.

Saumil Majmudar, the founder of SportzVillage, a company that is a clear market leader in youth sports management in the country, learnt this aspect at an extremely high price. Saumil does not shy away from the fact that his earlier venture was a failure, 'One of the learnings that I took from the failure was that if I had hung in there for some more time, the story would have been different. I got carried away with the notion that it was not big enough, that we had to do it within a certain time. QSupport was among the early players in the remote tech support businesses. After two years, the same space had companies hiring teams as big as 3,000–5,000. You have to look at solving the customer problem and build the business, rather than constantly benchmark yourself with your peers and batch-mates.'

I agree completely with Saumil's observation, I have seen many founders keen to pack up, not because the business isn't doing well, but because they believe they haven't scaled up fast enough as their institute peers have and as a result feel it is not worth their time.

WEAR YOUR PASSION ON YOUR SLEEVE

To be a successful entrepreneur, you must have the audacity to 'ask'. In a start-up, you are always asking people for something. You are asking your employees to buy into your vision and join you at reduced salaries, potential customers to buy your products, investors to back your vision and media to cover your story.

According to Phaneesh Murthy, who not only had a stellar sales career with Infosys but was a founder and investor in a number of businesses, 'A true founder is an evangelist of sorts, whether you are communicating with your customers, recruiting new employees, working to keep your current employees happy or talking to media. For entrepreneurs, there are no business hours. When you wear your passion for your business on your sleeve, it can be contagious and before you know it, the person you met by luck also happens to be in the market for exactly what you have to offer.'

The other trait that entrepreneurs need to inculcate within themselves is the ability to take rejections. Rejections and living through them are what make the life journey of a start-up founder. You will have to be able to take 'No' for an answer not only from a multitude of potential investors and customers you pitch to, but also from potential employees, who wouldn't buy into your vision and would refuse to be a co-passenger with you in the journey.

Rajat Mohanty, says 'If you are a founder, you are constantly trying to persuade others of your viewpoint. You are convincing buyers, investors, employees, partners, etc. at every stage. If you cannot articulate your vision, product and offering, then you cannot be successful. You cannot delegate this aspect. Even if you are a technical person, as a founder, you need to build such skills.'

SHARE THE BAD NEWS

A start-up founder is also the leader of the motley crew he has assembled around him, wedded to his passion and idea. He needs to be an optimist, yet he cannot exhibit the 'ostrich syndrome' and dig his head in the sand in the face of difficulty. He needs to be able to spot a problem early on and then honestly deliver the bad news to the crew and admit when things do not go as planned.

Founders must focus on solutions to problems but that doesn't mean they should 'fake it'—investors, employees and customers value honesty. It is only when the founder admits a mistake or a problem that they can get the teams and investors to rally together to find a solution. This doesn't come easily to a founder. Founders associate a business failure with themselves, as in the initial days they are synonymous with the company. This leads them to fake it or delay sharing the bad news, which can often drive the start-up to a point of no return. Says Rajat Mohanty, 'I have learnt that what helps when bad news arrives, is how quickly you can get the key people together and discuss a plan. There is no point in retreating into a shell.'

THRIVE IN CHAOS

Clearly understanding your strengths and what makes you really geared up is very important before you embark on this journey. There are many who fancy entrepreneurship but are inherently more comfortable in a structured environment. Professionally, they find it enjoyable when there is a well-defined path for them and when they have clearly defined roles. Instead of creating a new vision and plan, they tend to bring in efficiencies in already created ecosystems. If you are one such person, then do not get onto the start-up train. This journey is not meant to be for you.

To be a successful entrepreneur, you need to be able to, as the proverb goes, 'thrive in chaos'. Change is the only constant for an entrepreneur. Their plans are changed continuously, when they roll out their product and get customer feedback, when they are ready to launch but have reached the end of the runway of funding, when they review their marketing budget and realize they are short of funding or when they are suddenly slapped with a lawsuit over the infringement of certain patents in their product set.

In this start-up world, where nothing is definitive, the entrepreneur must survive and thrive. They must have the wherewithal to present a strategic long-term view of the business to a potential investor or partner, knowing well that after the meeting, they will have to speak to employees and request them to bear for a few days as the monthly salary will be delayed. This life of dichotomy and lack of any progressive planning is not for all and one needs to be aware of this prior to commencing the journey.

Entrepreneurs will only succeed when they are comfortable in their own skins. Get into entrepreneurship with your eyes wide open. 'Be aware of all the warts under the veneer of the start-up glamour' is my personal advice to all founders-to-be. And once you know entrepreneurship is your calling, know how to cross the Rubicon and start off on the journey.

BEING START-UP BATTLE READY

- Learn to embrace anonymity.
- Get complete support and backing from the family.
- Be comfortable in your own skin.
- Burn the bridge of escape.
- Learn to ask, but also be able to accept rejections.
- Accept and adapt to change and uncertainty.

2

CROSSING THE RUBICON IS SOMETIMES MORE DIFFICULT THAN THE BATTLE AHEAD

Once you are convinced that you have the DNA of an entrepreneur and you are not fazed by the journey, you need to make a move. One of the questions that I am frequently asked by those who want to embark on the entrepreneurial journey is 'how does one start?' Is there a 'eureka moment'? And if so, how does one recognize the eureka moment. Is it a flashpoint or a series of sequential events? Is it something that one has experienced oneself and hence, comes with the idea? Or is it an idea that someone pointed out? How long does one take to decide the right time to quit a job? Can one stay in their job and start the business?

There is, honestly, no definitive answer to these questions. So far, no one has been able to tell the 'right' time to start. But as Rajat Mohanty shares: 'There is a Chinese proverb that I like, "The best time to plant a tree was 20 years ago. The second-best time is now." If you have an idea and you are passionate about it, go for it. Unless you get head on into it, you won't know if it works.'

The fact is, there is never a bad time to launch a business. It is obvious why it is smart to launch when the economy is strong and growing. People have money and are looking for ways to spend it. Investors are in a more positive frame of mind. But launching in tough or uncertain economic times can be just as smart.

People believe starting a business is a mysterious process. They know they want to start a business, but they do not know the first steps to take.

Many people wonder if there is a good time to start their business idea.

Saumil Majmudar has an interesting take on the 'eureka moment'. The idea of SportzVillage came when a friend of Saumil's complained about how his child was not interested in physical activity and preferred to spend more time on the computer. 'The big learning for me, after two of my earlier ventures had failed, was that as an entrepreneur if you are solving a fundamental customer need, then you have a business. The model may differ but you still have a solid base,' he shared.

Between 2003–08, as he was building a sustainable and scalable business model around getting kids to play outside, Saumil tried almost five to six models, but none worked. In the sixth year, many people told him he was wasting time and that he should return to working in a corporate. 'But I stuck to it because I believe that if the fundamental customer problem is solved, then there must be a model. From then on, first, I stopped benchmarking myself to my batchmates and second, I removed the time horizon. Solving the problem became the focus. What happened then was that the first decision made me realize the issue was more like a cash-flow problem, which meant was I making enough for my own survival and for that I took up a consulting job, and the rest of the day would be utilized for my business. When you have the luxury of time, you start to think better. I was, and most of us are, stuck in this notion of limited time. I have to do this or that by this time. Time is probably the most effective but the most under-used weapon that an entrepreneur has,' said Saumil.

In 2007–08, they started approaching corporates and by 2009, two successful business models emerged—EduSports (now SportzVillage Schools), to help schools with an integrated, age-appropriate and structured Physical Education & Sports curriculum, and SportzConsult (SportzVillage XP) to help corporates achieve their branding and consumer engagement goals through Experiential Sports Marketing.

Saumil's story is an inspiring one and one that made me aware of the fact that, as entrepreneurs, we know what we want to do but it is the path that needs to be tread that matters. Although he had obstacles, Saumil was ready to refocus and plan better. When you are starting from ground zero, you have nothing to lose; just be flexible and ready to improvise.

THE FIRST STEPS

People's mental blocks prevent them from taking that crucial first step. Fear of the unknown paralyzes many before they can take the step. Others keep on rejecting ideas because they feel they are not new or unique. In reality, start-ups are not just about the newest and path-breaking technology products. It could well be about repurposing an existing technology for a newer and better use, devising a new business model that unlocks value or simply bringing a new product or service that already exists, to a newer region or to a new set of users at cheaper rates.

Take the case of my friend of over three decades, Sanjay Gaikwad, who built a business called UFO Moviez which was responsible for changing the film business in India. When he started the business in the mid-2000s, there were around 5000–6000 cinemas in India. In those days, film distribution used to happen using 35 mm reels and each reel would cost around ₹10 lakh. Even the biggest blockbuster movies in Bollywood or in South India would have about 200 of the old 35 mm reels which would pass on from one circuit to another. The movies would first be shown in the metros and then to the suburbs and finally to the tier 2 and tier 3 cities. The whole cycle of a film would take 3–4 months. This was a double whammy. If the movie was a success, pirated copies used to make their way to the tier 2 and tier 3 cities and if the movie failed, the cinema halls in remote circuits would cancel their orders.

Sanjay created a VSAT network across the country, connecting the cinema halls, and distributed digital scrambled signals straight to the cinemas. Using this, he could create a network of over 5,000 digital cinemas where, films could be released simultaneously across regions on the very first day. This has fundamentally changed the dynamics of the film industry in India and increased the total box office collection of the industry, enabling many more movies to come to market. He did not create any breakthrough technology. He merely used globally available technology to create a scalable and affordable solution that changed an entire industry.

Before starting UFO Moviez, Sanjay was busy selling infrastructure services for online lotteries and was making around ₹3 crore per day with more than 6,000 terminals on their network. But they were looking for an idea that could revolutionize the way movies are exhibited.

COOKING UP A PERFECT IDEA

How does a business idea come to a person? Again, there are no definite answers. Your idea could be related to the industry you are working in, or could be a product or service from a different area you are passionate about.

I remember having a chat with Sanjeev Kapoor, the celebrity chef and television personality, in 1995 at Juhu Centaur in Mumbai, where he was the executive chef, when I had asked him what his vision was for the future. He spoke of how 'cooking and food' is a passion for Indians and how there was a need for creating a business around the idea of a 'celebrity chef'. His show Khana Khazana had started to air on Zee TV in 1992.

One of the observations that he shared with me was that there was a growing consumer base of Indians who could not afford five-star dining but wanted five-star menus. According to him, the celebrity chef could bridge this gap. The chef could publish his recipes across various media like print, television and digital media. This was clearly ahead of its time and someone as optimistic as me had also thought that this was a figment of his wild imagination. Three decades later, he has executed his vision to the letter and spirit, and has stayed relevant to the changing consumer.

When I reminded him about our discussion and asked if he had planned this journey, Sanjeev said, 'In life we always want to have the best. Did I plan all this right at the time I started television? The answer is no.'

His transition from a celebrity chef to a businessman happened because he saw an opportunity at the right time and worked on it. For instance, the impact of influence and the need to connect with a wider audience-base happened accidently. 'I had just started Khana Khazana and was given a UK magazine to read. The magazine had published a six-part series on eggs by Chef Delia Smith and the article looked into how the consumption of eggs in the UK had gone up during that time. In one of the segments, while making an omelette, Delia had said, "Wow, this pan is a little gem, makes a perfect omelette." The sale of that pan went up by 440 per cent, claimed the article. The idea of selling cookware came from that. Of course the magazine was brought to me by a cookware brand who wanted me to do a similar endorsement. But what I saw in there was the impact of influence. That got to me and I started to use mediums other than TV to connect with people. Whether it was radio shows or writing columns in newspapers, magazines and websites...I did everything possible. As early as 1996, I had a website. I even started my own channel, FoodFood,' he says.

Similar is the story of WonderChef, his appliances business. In the US, George Foreman grills are extremely popular. The grill is promoted by the professional boxer George Foreman. A company wanted to bring these grills to India under the name Sanjeev Kapoor Tandoor. The product was instantly a big hit. This made Sanjeev realize the option of the appliances business. He also saw that there was a need and demand for such products. Today, the appliances business is around ₹300 crore in revenues.

Above all these bets, I think what Sanjeev has managed to achieve is to elevate the stature of chefs, who, till he started Khana Khazana, were relegated to the kitchens of five-star hotels with no identity of their own.

Ideas can emerge from areas that you are passionate about. Take the case of Aniruddha Sharma, founder and CEO Carbon Clean Solutions. He has been a strong climate change advocate and has been in favour of countries taking strict climate change measures. In 2009, at the United Nations Climate Change Conference held in Copenhagen, he was one of the protestors who had demanded that all countries sign up for a pledge to aggressively reduce their carbon footprint. Reducing industrial pollution matters to Aniruddha because he comes from Bhopal, which saw India's worst industrial disaster. 'Four days before the Bhopal gas leak happened, my entire family was in the city for my parents' marriage. I have seen up close the impact of the Bhopal Gas Tragedy on many of my family members and its continuing effects; no amount of medication can help. I do feel that something bad can happen if we do not control industrial pollution. This was just one city. Imagine if this had happened on a large scale,' he shared.

So, when his friend at IIT Kanpur, Prateek Bumb, started discussing his internship with an Italian professor on using technology to reduce carbon emission in industries, Aniruddha saw an opportunity for commercializing this idea. And over a cup of coffee between two friends, Carbon Clean Solutions was created.

Says Aniruddha, 'This was actually a coffee conversation I had with my co-founder Pratik. In 2008, Pratik was interning with a professor in Italy and they were looking at this technology. So, when I asked him if anybody was doing this in India, he said no one—that was the start of the company. We formed a team, started participating in inter-IIT business competitions and at the first pan-IIT business conclave, we received the first award and it came from Tata Motors and Tata Steel. At that award function, both the Tata CEOs said, "If you can solve this problem, we will be your first customers." That made us think—if two of the most respected companies of the country are interested in what we are doing, then we are on the right path.' That was how Carbon Clean Solutions began and today, they have moved their operations to London and raised over $26 million. What started out of passion for clean environment has developed into a large global business that provides cleantech solutions to large enterprises globally.

Sometimes, a recurring problem one faces germinates an idea, which in turn becomes an opportunity. The seed of Redbus was sown in the entrepreneurial ground in 2005, when Phanindra (Phani) Sama, an engineer in a multinational at the time, was going to travel from Bangalore to Hyderabad for his Diwali vacations, and he missed the bus. Says Phani, the founder of Redbus, 'I could not get a bus ticket to travel to my hometown. I wandered around Bangalore for a ticket. That day I came to know the disorganization in the system and the communication gap between bus operators and travel agents. There was no transparency on the availability of seats and ticket prices, and everything was done through phone calls.' Phani found the whole process clumsy and fragmented. 'I believed the problem could be solved through an online platform. Then I discussed with my friends and three of us got together and decided to become entrepreneurs, more driven by the idea and opportunity, than by the hangover of wanting to be an entrepreneur.'

The business idea could be based on a global business model and you could roll it out in your home market and be a success. Bhavesh Agarwal was with Microsoft Research when he had a bad experience in a cab journey in 2011, and started Ola Cabs, replicating the Uber model which had started in the US in 2009.

What Bhavesh and Ankit Bhati, his co-founder, did was to enhance the Uber model for the Indian context. They added premium pricing and provided Wi-Fi and in-screen services which appealed to always-ON, data-hungry Indians. Given that India did not have public toilets like the west, Ola mapped out in their apps, the nearest toilets. They started the famed OTP (one-time password) to ensure only the right customer could take the booked cab and not someone else, intentionally or otherwise. All this planning elevated the plain vanilla Uber model to a different level in India. There is no harm in creating a business around a global business model if it is customized for the home market, and executed to perfection and scale.

IDEAS ARE CHEAP

In today's world, ideas are not proprietary. I have often seen founders be extremely secretive, even bordering on paranoia, about their idea. I remember a call with a very bright young lady who had built a product using Artificial Intelligence (AI) to better beauty and health products by creating smarter products around personalization, with feedback and insights. I thought she had a good value proposition and when she pitched for funding, I readily agreed.

It was during the COVID pandemic and we were in lockdown, so I couldn't meet her in person. We decided to hold the pitch over a WebEx call. Things were fine when she began her pitch process. As I began to ask her pointed questions, wanting to know more about the product, I could sense a growing nervousness in her. When I started making notes, she became jittery and after pitching for 20-odd minutes, she said she was uncomfortable talking about it without an NDA, as she felt the idea could be copied. Little did she realize that no investor signs NDAs for basic pitches. Further, all she was talking about was 'an idea'. If one is overly protective about an idea, worried that someone might 'steal the idea' and execute it better; then the idea is already frail, with no moats to protect the business and is easily replicable.

It is understandable that founders are like new parents. They fall in love with the start-up babies as soon as they conceive them. As soon as the idea is born, they want to protect it and keep it in a protective bubble, away from the rest of the world lest it catches an infection.

On the contrary, one has to expose the babies to the outside world to strengthen their immune system and make them world-ready. The same is true for start-ups. As soon as you are certain you want to pursue an idea, instead of being secretive about it, you have to be out and testing your thesis, talking to industry professionals and even others in the market to gauge if your idea has wings, and if you can build a business out of the same.

Coming up with an idea is just 10 per cent of the work. The next step is to build a story around your start-up idea. Investors, employees and customers buy the story and vision associated with it. What is the type of company you are looking to create? What is the pain-point you are trying to solve? Who is it for? Is your product a good to have or a must-have offering?

Think of the business you are trying to create in holistic and strategic terms. Often, a founder gets caught in minutiae and in over-detailing a process—losing the big picture. I have seen many a technology-led founders get caught in the romance of the technology that they are creating and unable to articulate the strategic intent of the business. I guess that is where a founding team comes into play—where a business-oriented and a nuts-and-bolts person work together and complement each other.

Genrobotics is a portfolio company of Unicorn India Ventures. It is a robotics company which provides a number of critical solutions for society. One of the robots they have built, 'Bandicoot', is being used to eradicate manual scavenging. Says Vimal Govind, the CEO and co-founder of the business, 'As students, we were driven by two things—robotics and social service. During the college years, four of us were actively involved with the National Service Scheme (NSS) and other social services. The impact of this was that for all the college projects, our subjects would be driven towards the use of technology to solve social problems.' As a result, when real-life threw a problem at them they knew how to go about it.

An incident in Calicut where three people died in a manhole made these four engineer friends give up their engineering jobs and employ their robotics skill towards solving this problem. 'A manual scavenger was killed when he got trapped in the manhole he was cleaning, and two other people died trying to rescue him. It was a shocking incident; it made us wonder that even today after so much development people are dying doing such menial work. This gave us a purpose and passion to use our technology for a commercial and social cause, and not restrict it to the laboratories. We came together to create Genrobotics,' says Vimal. Today Genrobotics is successfully working with several Smart City projects and state governments.

ANALYSIS PARALYSIS

The other tricky part of kicking off a start-up is how to approach the same. If it were a traditional product launch of a large company, one would do focused group and deep market research. These would enhance the success rate and provide confidence for a launch. That is what we learned in the annals of classical management. However, these do not hold true for the start-up world.

The uncertainty of the start-ups, unpredictability of the business model and lack of clarity of the customer's reactions make it difficult to undertake research and if undertaken, it's difficult for the research to hold water.

This leads to some founders being too instinct-oriented and who say, 'Let's just get on with it.' While this plays to the entrepreneurial impulse, having been involved with so many start-ups, I think this is a recipe for disaster. Before these founders realize it, they are too far down the path without any feedback loop, deluding themselves into thinking they know what the customer wants.

While this is one extreme, on the other extreme are founders who spend incessant hours talking to customers, reading myriads of research reports and strategizing their ideas prior to the launch. They are caught in the classical 'analysis-paralysis mode' and they too will not know what the future holds, as the patterns in a start-up are unpredictable.

What then is the best form to launch products and services in a start-up. Can one have a method in the manic world of start-up madness? How does one attempt to reduce the failure rates? We cover some of these aspects in the next chapter, which entails how, from day one, one can plan so as to enhance the mortality rate of the start-up.

BEING START-UP BATTLE READY

- There is no perfect time to start; it is all in the mind.
- Don't search for the most innovative idea; find a problem that you feel your idea solves.
- Don't be afraid to replicate proven models as long as you can execute them better.
- Don't be caught up in minutiae; consider the big picture.
- Don't be secretive and paranoid about your idea.
- Plan ahead but don't be caught in analysis-paralysis.

3

PLAN BEFORE YOU LEAP, BUT TRUST YOUR INTUITION WHEN YOU DO

START SMALL AND FOCUS ON EXECUTION

Having crossed the 'Rubicon', it is now time for one to plan ahead. Every multibillion-dollar business starts small. But the big question that an entrepreneur needs to grapple with early on is whether the idea can become a scalable business proposition or if it is just a hobbyhorse for the entrepreneur.

I recently came across a bright team of experienced media professionals who were building a new OTT (over-the-top) platform, like Netflix, for Bengali content. When I brought up competition, they stated their business model was unique, as they were the only ones to provide dedicated Bengali content to those living outside West Bengal. And they were adamant about it. They had not taken into account that Bengali content is available on Netflix and Amazon Prime, and for free on YouTube.

For a viewer, the positioning and the technology used to deliver the content has no relevance, as they can access content on any platform. Also, OTT platforms are fighting among themselves for a share of eyeballs, with tough competition from global players like Netflix and Amazon. The team had not understood their business environment and the competitive sphere in the minds of their end consumer, and had pitch-forked themselves to an unscalable niche. By claiming they were 'in a league of their own' they had established in my mind that there was indeed no league where they could play.

But they are not the first ones to do so. One of the intriguing answers I often hear from start-up founders when asked about market potential is that 'there is no competition' or 'we are in a league of our own'. This for me is the most off-putting answer. If you say there is no competition, it either means you are in a niche that isn't scalable or you haven't understood the market, or both.

One must start small and focus on execution, work towards measurable offering and take a leadership into that realm. But the vision of the entrepreneur must be the larger play, else, the market size becomes very constricted and businesses cannot scale. *'What is the business I am in and who is my competition?'* The answer must be clear in the mind of the founder.

In this context, the story of Paladion is worth sharing. Rajat Mohanty, the founder says, 'When we launched, our aim was to first capture the India market. The other aspect was our approach—we were looking at the smallest market that we could dominate and create an identity of being the best in that market. And we also wanted to do this in an economical manner. We were clear from day one that this was the start-up strategy. We wanted to play in the global space and build scale but only after we dominated in one market.'

ANALOGS AND ANTILOGS

Silicon Valley lawyer-turned-venture capital (VC) investor Randy Komisar touched upon the concept of analogs and antilogs[1] in *Getting to Plan B*. Analogs are those companies in the same industry that you seek to do business in or from a different industry that has a similar business model. Antilogs are the opposite—organizations you do not want to replicate from. While your business model may be a new one, it is important to understand the analogs and antilogs of your business.

---

[1]John Walker Mullins and Randy Komisar. *Getting to Plan B: Breaking through to a Better Business Model.* Harvard Business Press, 2010.

Antilogs and Analogs help clarify the early thought-processes of entrepreneurs.

As discussed earlier, many founders are of the opinion that in the absence of historical data, they can just go ahead and see what happens. They like to play blind. While entrepreneurship is about believing in oneself, I think, there is also a need to follow certain best practices that help increase the chances of success.

In the UK, LaundryApp, a high-end laundry delivery service, has been a success story. Vishal Kothari, a young entrepreneur, had availed of this service when he used to live in the UK. Upon returning to India, he was keen to recreate it in the country and came to me. This was in 2016, when the numbers of on-demand services were mushrooming in India. This was also the time when home-delivered beauty and spa services and on-demand multi-service platforms like UrbanClap and Housejoy were making a mark. Vishal had worked out that these businesses were the analogs of the business he was looking to build. Urban middle-class folks were hard-pressed for time and were looking at pre-booking slots at home for various household services.

But he had not considered the antilogs of the business. Laundry services were too localized and the street corner dhobi was difficult to displace. Even laundry chains like German Laundry could not scale up and displace the local dhobi. Also, he had not worked out that the aggregation model of dhobis wouldn't work as these were, more often than not, daily services, unlike services involving beauty technicians and AC mechanics, which were generally on-demand-based and episodic. These were the antilogs of his business and I had articulated the same to him. Because he had discounted the antilogs and was drawing comfort from the analogs, he went ahead and launched his business.

Unfortunately, he could not scale up the business even after getting angel funding and had to shut. Later when I met Vishal, he was gracious enough to accept my earlier comments and has now gone on to build a successful business in fintech, having taken learnings from his past experiences.

THE KORAMANGALA ECHO CHAMBER SYNDROME

An experienced founder must step outside their comfort zone and engage with as many of his potential consumers directly to get their feedback. He must be able to deconstruct the intermediary layers and talk directly to the customers. This is also true for business-to-business (B2B) founders, who need to remember that even if they are selling to large enterprises, at the end of the day, there is an individual on the other side who will be the enterprise's champion. It is, therefore, important to spend time with the end users and get to know them, their pain points and what exactly they are trying to solve.

In Bengaluru, the start-up hub of the country, an interesting phenomenon has emerged—the 'Koramangala Syndrome'. Koramangala, the amicable neighbourhood of Bengaluru has become the hot-spot of start-ups. Many a start-up founder and investor can be found in the locality's Starbucks, Café Coffee Day, Costa Coffee and Third Wave Coffee Roasters. Whenever I meet start-up founders and they explain to me that they have got market feedback, I ask them if they are suffering from the 'Koramangala Syndrome'. For me, this reflects a natural inclination of founders to keep doing market reality check from 'PLU' (people like us) and to live in an echo-chamber, convincing themselves that a market exists.

Successful founders go into their markets and get feedback along the way and finetune their value proposition. Take the case of Abhishek Negi, whom Unicorn India Ventures had backed in his first venture in the mobility space; unfortunately the business had to close within a couple of years. I spoke to him after a few years and discovered that he has built a successful, well-funded business in agri-tech. I naturally asked him how he came up with the idea. His clarity of thinking and the quick lessons he picked up from the market impressed me.

Abhishek shared, 'One thing was clear to me at the time of starting up again—the next business has to have a large enough set of problems (from a sector scale), positive high unit margins (for ongoing sustenance and no reliance on external capital), less competition (major focus during initial days should be in building a defensible product/service and not competing with others) and the founding team's mindset has to be nimble and aggressive. I've always been interested in large enough problems, especially in India, where the solutions can have a profound disruptive impact on a sector and create value for all stakeholders.'

He went on to say, 'We were sure that we wanted to do something in the agritech space, but we were not sure as to what we want to do because none of us has an agriculture background. However, we all believe that the agri space is at the cusp of rapid growth. With widespread 4G rollout in 2017, growing awareness among consumers for healthy food and understanding about the sector from an insider point of view, got me to a conviction that the agri sector is, in fact, the right sector.' Eggoz, his present venture, was the fourth pivot idea, where he found all of the above criteria. The idea was finally fleshed out after a year of conversations with people involved in agri-trade throughout India. Eggoz works with poultry farmers and uses nutritional engineering and technology to produce high quality and nutrition-rich eggs.

Abhishek had drawn lessons from the failure of his first venture. Instead of being the 'let's just do it' entrepreneur, he had matured into someone who wanted to spend time in defining the market, get feedback from the community and pivot the business plan, prior to launching the business full scale. All of these are the building blocks for a long-term sustainable business.

Entrepreneurship is about learning every day. Going to the drawing board every time to hone your business will only make it more adaptable and also reduce risk. When you start, you have little to show, but as you continue taking steps, you get that much closer to your goals.

FIRST-MOVER DISADVANTAGE

Another area of feedback is learning from the competitive landscape. It is sometimes better for the founders to go slow, let the markets mature and then go all out. The market development and learnings can thus be made at the expense of someone else. It is not always about who the first one to launch is, instead it is about the first one to execute in a sustainable manner.

Al Ries and Jack Trout came up with the management philosophy of 'first-mover advantage' in *The 22 Immutable Laws of Marketing*.[2] When the book was written, in 1994, the network effects weren't as viral as they are today; one didn't have the ability to reconsider their options with the touch of a phone button and innovation wasn't a constant process of evolution like today. But in today's dog-eat-dog world of start-ups, it is more often the later movers who have an inherent advantage. Learning from early movers, enables a later-mover founder to take advantage of the market development, customer education and awareness, infrastructure development and also, strong reference data points to take meaningful decisions.

Let us take the case of Udaan, a B2B e-commerce platform and India's fastest unicorn business. All the three founders Vaibhav Gupta, Sujeet Kumar and Amod Malviya were part of Flipkart's core team when the e-commerce giant scaled out, and it helped them in the scaleup at Udaan.

Says Amod, 'There was lot of learning between balancing growth and stability. There is always a tussle between the two—if you are expanding fast, then the base on which you are expanding is not robust enough, but if you compromise growth then you lose market share. Balancing these is an art, something which we do not excel in, as of now. What worked in our favour was that we saw a lot of these things at Flipkart, the initial team at Udaan had seen scaleout at Flipkart. Anybody who has gone through a scaleout curve tends to anticipate problems. There were a lot of mistakes we were able to avoid because of our Flipkart experience.'

FORESEEING AN OPPORTUNITY

In some cases, the opportunity is so obvious that one does not need validation to start the business. It is about imagining how one can better or improve a solution or service.

Rajesh Jain was India's first internet entrepreneur and created IndiaWorld (IW) at a time when India had no start-up culture and no net connectivity. IW happened because after coming back from the US,

[2]Al Ries and Jack Trout. *The 22 Immutable Laws of Marketing: Violate Them at Your Own Risk*. Harper Business, 1994.

Rajesh had tried his hand at a few things, but they all failed. On one of his visits to the US, he realized it was very hard to get the latest news/ information of what was happening in India. Indian papers and magazines would take at least a week or two to reach the US. The backdrop of foreseeing an opportunity came from the pain point he faced and the fact that the internet was making its presence felt in the US. In his words, 'I realized early on that the internet could be the bridge, and my early words were, "It could become an electronic information marketplace." That is how this idea started.'

Says Rajesh, of foreseeing an opportunity and grasping it: 'The fact that I failed in my earlier entrepreneurial stints, also meant I *had* to succeed. I say this because, if my earlier stints would have been successful, I would not have been focused on IW. The problem that I wanted to solve came to me because of my own experiences. In the early days of the internet, my idea was based on something new that could be created. I had no idea how big it would be.'

But everyone may not experience a pain point which can turn into a business idea. How does one then foresee an opportunity? Rajesh opines that, 'There is an "outside" in view, where you are looking at the market potential, customers, people and thinking how to better a service or product. An entrepreneur is one who finds better ways to solve problems.'

BUILD-MEASURE-LEARN SPRINTS

Eric Ries in his famed book *The Lean Start-up*[3] defines the concept of the minimum viable product (MVP) and how it can help start-ups avoid wasting their effort and time. MVP helps entrepreneurs start the process of learning as quickly as possible. It isn't necessarily the simplest prototype, but is the fastest way to get through the Build-Measure-Learn feedback loop with minimum effort and costs.

One of the challenges first-time entrepreneurs face with MVP is that they assume early adapters of the MVP will not be able to comprehend

---

[3]Eric Ries. *The Lean Start-up: How Constant Innovation Creates Radically Successful Businesses*. Penguin Business, 2019.

the entire offering and reject it. They are also apprehensive of showing the MVP to investors, lest the investors opt out of it. While their fears are not unfounded, the founders need to have confidence in the MVP and should be able to articulate how the MVP fits in the big scheme of things.

When I started Recreate Solutions in 2000, the cost of starting a technology business was much higher than it is today. Technology infrastructure was far more expensive as there was a need for dedicated connectivity, server farms and software. Today with cloud computing and distributed models of development, the cost of starting a technology business is negligible. Additionally, to 'catch them young,' players like Amazon, Google and Microsoft have introduced various schemes that a start-up can avail to lower their storage and computing costs.

In these scenarios, it is important for the start-ups to be 'agile' and make changes in their products based on customer feedbacks. This agility is very different from the product development cycles of the yore. Now product development cycles are literally in sprints—Build-Measure-Learn sprints.

I strongly recommend having a detailed video of the entire service or product set, which a lot of founders successfully use alongside the MVP. By doing this, the founders get a quick feedback and are simultaneously able to hold the interest of early adapters and potential investors.

The analog-antilog analysis, feedback from the market and lessons from the first movers provide a strong framework for the entrepreneurs' decision-making. However, eventually, it is the intuition or the gut instinct of the entrepreneur that makes the difference.

As Oprah Winfrey has said, 'Learning to trust your instincts, using your intuitive sense of what's best for you, is paramount for any lasting success. I've trusted the still, small voice of intuition my entire life. And the only time I've made mistakes is when I didn't listen.'

BEING START-UP BATTLE READY

- Define the overall market you are playing in, but launch in a microcosm you wish to dominate.
- Look out for historical data through antilogs and analogs.
- Go out of your comfort zone and research the entire market, and not merely the early adapters.
- Learn from those who have launched before you.
- Make small mistakes and launch MVP; create a constant agile feedback loop using 'build-measure-learn sprints'.
- Use data and research as validation points and trust your entrepreneurial gut.

4

IT IS A LONELY RIDE,
PICK YOUR CO-PASSENGER WELL

It was Sachin Bansal and Binny Bansal who made Flipkart, Bill Gates and Paul Allen who created Microsoft and William Procter and James Gamble who started P&G. Of course, there is Jeff Bezos who is a sole founder and created Amazon.

Like in a marriage, it is important that you spend meaningful time with your co-founder before embarking on the entrepreneurial journey. The alignment of values, dreams and ambitions is critical, but it isn't enough for a start-up marriage to succeed. One of the key questions that needs to be addressed right at the inception is why he/she wants to get into entrepreneurship? Different people have different motivations for getting into business. Hence, you need to choose carefully while taking on a co-founder for this journey or selecting the A-team. Co-founders need to have similar objectives for successfully embarking on the entrepreneurial journey.

I cannot stress this factor more as I learnt this truth the hard way. I had started my first venture Recreate Solutions with a senior of mine from IIT Kharagpur, Neil Basu. After a hiatus of over a decade since we left the campus, we connected again in London. At the time, I was running the UK business of Alta Vista and he was an investment banker with a large European bank.

These were the heady days of 1999–2000, when the Nasdaq was having a one-way ride upwards! Between 1990 and 1997, in the developed economies, computer ownership had progressed from a luxury to a necessity. This was the beginning of the Information Age. At the same time, a decline in interest rates increased the availability of capital.

As a result of these factors, many investors were eager to invest, at any valuation, in any dot-com company, especially if it had one of the Internet-related prefixes or a '.com' suffix in its name. Venture capital was easy to raise. A combination of rapidly increasing stock prices in the technology sector and confidence that the companies would turn future profits created an environment in which many investors were willing to overlook traditional metrics, such as the price-earnings ratio, and base their confidence on technological advancements, leading to a stock market bubble.

Between 1995 and 2000, the Nasdaq Composite stock market index rose 400 per cent[4]. At the height of the boom, it was possible for a promising dot-com company to become a public company via an IPO and raise a substantial amount of money, even if it had never made a profit—in some cases, even if it had never realized any material revenue.

Bankers, fund managers and consultants were all leaving their professions and joining the tech ride in order to make 'untold millions'. Against this global backdrop, in India, the first global venture capital firms started to make their debut. And within India, there was a mushrooming of start-ups.

While working for AltaVista, I saw the roll-out of broadband; content was needed to feed the pipes. Most content then existed in legacy forms and there was a need to digitize and make the legacy content ready for the web. I was sure there was potential for a business to be built here.

I discussed the business with Neil for over six months and we decided to start a business called Recreate Solutions. While Neil had an appreciation of the business, he was a quintessential banker and was driven by the valuation and excitement in the global markets, at that point in time, towards technology business.

Both of us retained our respective jobs; with a business plan in place, we raised money from one of the early venture funds in India, Connect Capital. It was a $3 million funding, which was substantial in those days

---

[4] Vishal Noel. 'The Dot-Com Bubble of 2001.' *Medium*, 17 January 2020, medium.com/@vishalnoel7/the-dot-com-bubble-of-2001-18bf817abcbd. Accessed 21 November 2020.

and we began our journey in November 2000.

We went through the grime of building the operations in Mumbai and our sales team in London, and devising the value proposition for our customers. As is expected in any start-up, the journey was fraught with challenges and we were struggling to define the value proposition. And then came the summer of 2001. We realized that having built the organization, we needed to raise money to keep the growth going. While I was running shop, Neil took upon himself, being a banker, to raise the next round of funding.

Then 9/11 happened. Within days, as we became aware of the extent of the catastrophe that it had caused to human life and the global markets, we realized that we wouldn't be able to raise the funding we were looking for. Both of us reacted differently.

I immediately went onto a mission mode; spoke to investors, addressed the teams in all the regions and immediately embarked on a cost rationalization programme, and reduced the fixed costs by 70 per cent to extend the survival runway. Neil on the other hand, realized that without the commensurable funding, we wouldn't be able to scale the business in the time frame he had in mind, and he bailed out within a month and went back to banking.

While we are still in touch and Neil has had a successful career in financial services and runs a hedge fund, the relationship was never the same again.

This real-life example showed me that co-founders must have similar objectives when they start a business together. While both of us, undoubtedly, wanted to make financial returns out of the start-up, for me it was also to fulfill my dream of creating a media services business. I don't think Neil had such motivations.

Like most new founders, I too had made the mistake of taking on a co-founder with whom I would like to share a joke and a beer. One tends to go for co-founders who are mirror reflections of oneself, as this provides some personal comfort. But having a co-founder who is identical is fraught with problems. The clash of egos and personae as well as the overlap in skillsets and rolodex become friction points, even among the best of friends.

Among co-founders, it is all fine while the going is good; but despite the best intentions, co-founders can drift apart. This happens more so, when companies scale up and there are full-bloom executive teams. Some co-founders want to return to the start-up world and not run larger enterprises. This is usually true for tech founders, like Paul Allen or Steve Wozniak, who left the companies they had co-founded and nurtured.

In this context, it is important to have pre-nuptial co-founder contracts. At the time of founding, this is something that is not in the minds of the co-founders, but as an early-stage investor, Unicorn India Ventures insists on this. This protects everyone and most of all, the company. During the hard discussions driven by company lawyers, co-founders get a peek into what the future might hold for them.

A PARTNER IN TIME

Peter Thiel in *Zero to One* says, 'A start-up messed up in the foundation cannot be fixed.'[5] Termed Thiel's Law, it stresses upon the importance of a start-up's strong foundation. One of the most important pillars of this foundation is the relationship between the members of the founding team.

Being a start-up founder is a lonely position. While you will, over a period in time, have a team and investors, you can't share your emotions and problems openly with them. The only person you can be open with is your co-founder. According to me, finding the right co-founder is the most important, initial decision a founder must take.

Whenever someone asks me if they need a co-founder, my unequivocal response is 'Yes'. Unicorn India Ventures tends not to invest in businesses which have sole founders, as the risk of such businesses is very high.

As in any relationship, co-founders too need to figure out their space and comfort zone for the smooth functioning of a company. Initially, amongst co-founders, like in all relationships, there is optimism and camaraderie. Slowly, you start to notice the shortcomings in each other and the relationship starts getting strained. There are numerous instances

---

[5]Peter Thiel and Blake Masters. *Zero to One: Notes on Startups, or How to Build the Future.* Virgin Books, 2014.

where irreconcilable differences between the members of the founding team have led to the eventual erosion of value of the company.

The story of how the co-founders of BigBasket came together is an interesting one. In 2010, Abhinay Choudhari had started ShopasUlike, an online grocery service. Shortly after this, one of his friends joined him. Says Abhinay: 'But this friend of mine left within a few months as he was uncomfortable with the idea of not having a regular salary. The risks in running a start-up are very high. Running a company is difficult; there are just too many things happening and you need as many hands on the deck as possible and having co-founders helps in the operations of the business. Also, the sharing of ideas and experience is of importance in operations. I reached out to V.S. Sudhakar, who had been the CEO of Fabmart in 2000 and with whom I had been in touch during my first aborted business, in 2001.'

This time around, Abhinay roped in co-founders who had an earlier experience in ecommerce—he got the founders of Fabmart to join him. But the Fabmart founders did not join immediately. When Abhinay had approached Sudhakar in 2010, both he and Vipul Parekh were mentoring start-ups, hence they agreed to mentor Abhinay as well and would meet once a week for a token stake in the company. This arrangement went on for a year.

'In 2011, K. Ganesh, serial entrepreneur and promoter, approached Sudhakar and said that the online grocery segment was growing, and that he wanted to do something in that space. Sudhakar told them about me and that's how K. Ganesh, Meena Ganesh and Srinivas Anumolu came on board as promoters and brought in some financial capital. Sudhakar and Vipul also brought in the other two co-founders of Fabmart,' says Abhinay. That is how co-founder Abhinay Choudhari, V.S. Sudhakar, Vipul Parekh, Hari Menon and V.S. Ramesh came together.

JUGALBANDI

'Everything started as nothing' is the purest concept or summary of any start-up story, and I also believe that this journey is best experienced with a partner.

The complementarity of co-founders in terms of skillsets and mindset is key. Pankit Desai and Anand Naik, co-founders Sequretek, a cybersecurity player and a Unicorn India Venture invested firm, are the apt representation of co-founders. Both are seasoned professionals, of a similar age group and have spent over two decades in technology. So, to an outsider, their characteristics may seem identical, but they are a perfect complement for each other.

Pankit is gregarious by nature and a social creature, while Anand is the quieter one who absorbs all data points before opining. Emotionally also, they complement each other. Given the roller coaster rides start-ups take, co-founders need to have different diversity quotient levels. Pankit is always either at an emotional high or low, while I have seen Anand to be phlegmatic and always restrained. Their 'jugalbandi' has had a cooling impact on the investors and the executive team around them, and has helped to scale up the business in the face of competition and adverse market conditions.

My partner at Unicorn India Ventures, Anil Joshi, and I are like chalk and cheese. Anyone who knows us is surprised that we could have partnered and created one of India's foremost early-stage investment platform in less than five years. Not only are our personalities and backgrounds different but so are our skill-sets.

I am far from a detailed person when it comes to any commercial or shareholder contracts. Anil on the other hand, goes through contracts with a hair-comb. Every contract in the Fund, including those for companies I am on the board of, Anil drives to closure. There is no question of territorial power, but complete faith and understanding in what the other co-founder brings to the table.

TO BE OR NOT TO BE CEO

The most important trait in a co-founding relationship, like in a marriage, is honesty and the ability to share thoughts with each other. This journey is fraught with hardships and co-founders must feel comfortable enough to discuss everything with each other. This transcends matters related to the start-up and they must also be able to discuss personal issues.

In a start-up, the personal lives of the co-founders are interwoven with the journey of the start-up and it is exceedingly important that they be able to discuss the triumphs and tribulations of their lives with each other. In short, there should be no surprises to one another, as it would jolt the relationship and therein impact the start-up adversely.

Another important aspect of the co-founders' relationship are the roles and responsibilities. In the initial days of the start-up, roles and titles do not matter, as everyone is involved in everything—from defining the product, making the sales call, setting up the investor deck and meetings, managing the hires—they are joined at the hip. Slowly, as the company grows and newer members join the team, it becomes crucial for co-founders to clearly demarcate the roles and responsibilities. Doing so provides a clear direction to the co-founders and also gives a sense of purpose to the team.

One of the tasks co-founders, especially those who have been friends and are from a similar age group, struggle with is to define who will be the CEO of the business. This isn't easy, as CEOs need to be the first among equals. All co-founders have similar share-holding and contribute equally with their blood, toil, sweat and tears, yet only one is designated as the CEO. I would recommend that the CEO decision should be sorted out before you venture out to meet investors. It is always beneficial if the decision is unanimous rather than forced by a third party.

A simple way to solve this is to select the person who exhibits leadership quality. No one, especially among the co-founder's team, will listen to a CEO unless they are the clear leader and set the strategic agenda for the start-up. I have come across this challenge in many a start-up and have seen co-founders unwilling to bell the cat. Before investing, I insist on a clear organogram outside of the shareholding for everyone's clarity.

Genrobotics was started by four young engineers just out of college, as part of their robotics project. Unicorn India was the first investor in the team. The company has grown in the last three years and has secured external funding as well. For us to work with the founding team and clearly assign Vimal the role of the CEO was quite a task, but the entire team was very co-operative. Vimal has clearly stepped up to the task and taken to the leadership bestowed on him by the investors and co-founders.

However, like always, there are successful exceptions to this rule.

The case study of Udaan, a B2B marketplace, is interesting. The founders have decided not to have designations like CEO. Says Amod Malviya, 'We decided to stay away from designations. This allows us to solve problems without artificial constraints that come with role definitions. For example, if Vaibhav [Gupta] thinks of a new product category then he need not rely on anyone, he can move independently. Essentially it allows for lesser interweaving. By not having titles and turning on high level of trust we can move in parallel. In hindsight, I think this has been one of the significant reasons for our scaleup.' Amod feels that since all the three founders have worked together, they understand each other's strengths and weaknesses.

This decision has had its impact on Udaan too because investors prefer to have a clearly defined path. 'There was one investor whom we met, who liked us a lot and spent a good 40–45 minutes discussing our platform, but at the end of it, he asked who the CEO was and we said we do not have that designation. He told us they do not invest in companies that do not have a clearly defined CEO. I think a lot of people tend to perceive such a leadership team as indecisive. We think in a different way,' shared Amod.

The founders of Udaan believe that the traditional structure creates a unidimensional leadership. Their reasoning is that no single person has all the required capabilities to solve a problem. Again, this is something that they had observed in Flipkart and made sure to not make the same mistakes. 'This is something we saw at Flipkart too, when you, as a leader, are making decisions about things that you do not understand, there are moments when it will be okay because you have trust, but there will be moments when a decision is being taken because someone says so. And this tends to happen when there is a very fast-moving, high-pressure setup. We think, let the right person take the decision. There have been times when we have asked someone much closer to the customer to take a decision,' explained Amod.

◆

Another aspect I want founders to think about is having a mentor. The Indian start-up system does not talk about the importance of mentors, but there are successful founders who vouch for the role of a mentor. It is a well-known fact that Steve Jobs had mentors at various stages of life. He also mentored Mark Zuckerberg when Facebook was facing an existential crisis in the mid-2000s.

Closer home, successful entrepreneurs like Naveen Tewari of InMobi was helped by Harvard Business School professor Tarun Khanna, and Lenskart's Peyush Bansal has been counseled by Ratan Tata.

Sanjay Anandaram, who has spent over three decades as an entrepreneur, corporate executive, venture capitalist, angel investor, teacher, advisor and mentor, and who has been a mentor to Phanindra Sama of Redbus, believes that mentors in India having a mentor on board of a start-up is not a decision that entrepreneurs make regularly. However, he feels that there is a lot more appreciation of the fact that having a mentor can have a positive impact on the founder/CEO.

The distinction between a mentor and a consultant or advisor isn't clear or obvious to many founders and CEOs. There are no watertight distinctions and the roles often diffuse and merge. Sanjay likes to draw the analogy of Krishna in Mahabharata to differentiate between these three roles. A consultant is brought in when there is a specific problem that needs resolution, within a specific time frame. For instance, when you need to create the HR payroll system in the company, the consultants design and implement the system within a specified time period. In the Mahabharata, Bheema locked in combat with the equally powerful Jarasandha, looks to Krishna for help. Now Krishna, who knew the story of Jarasandha's birth, picked up a twig from the floor, broke it in two halves and threw the two halves far away from each other. Bheema now knew what had to be done. He threw Jarasandha to the ground, held his legs and split his body in two. He then threw the two halves of Jarasandha far away from each other, so that they might not join. Krishna in this scenario acts as a consultant who delivers a specific solution to a specific problem at the required time.

An entrepreneur requires an advisor when no clear-cut solution is visible, and an understanding of the overall context, coordination with stakeholders and execution is required to solve a challenging situation. Again, during the Kurukshetra war, when the question of killing Bheeshma arises, Krishna tells Arjuna that it could be accomplished with the help of Shikhandi, who had been born a woman. The Pandavas however, were unsure and reluctant. Krishna convinced Arjuna to have Shikhandi in front of him, on his chariot, while battling Bheeshma who, thanks to a vow he had made, would not fight any woman or any man who had been a woman. Arjuna was then able to fell Bheeshma. In this situation, Krishna played the role of an advisor using his knowledge, understanding of the situation and persuasiveness to convince Arjuna and the Pandavas to follow a course of action.

A mentor is a superset of a consultant and an advisor. His relationship with the founder is to be a sounding board, friend, philosopher, coach, guide and confidant. The role of Krishna in motivating and inspiring Arjuna to see the big picture, to focus on his dharma and fight the great battle, when he was overcome with emotion and distraught at the prospect of fighting his kith and kin, is what a mentor does at times of doubt, lack of confidence and emotional dilemma. 'This is a relationship which is built on mutual trust and confidence. The founder needs to have an open mind, not be bogged down by ego and understand that the mentor is there to support him think through solutions during difficult times. Issues such as dealing with team conflicts, departures of key employees, relationships with board members, and many other emotionally stressful ones are when a founder can benefit enormously by having a mentor,' explains Sanjay.

Mentors are generally people who have been entrepreneurs and who can help founders to take informed decisions based on their experience.

As finding the correct co-founder is important, getting access to a good mentor who can be your guide and philosopher in this journey will be an added advantage.

FAMILY MATTERS

Sometimes, co-founders may also be family members, spouses, siblings or parent and child. The journey of co-founders is anyway akin to walking over egg-shells, having a relative in the same team adds to the complications. Most investors avoid co-founders being related parties.

There are number of reasons for the same. First, when a decision has to be made, you want the founders to make the best decision for the business, even when the decision may not favorably affect the relationship. However, when family members are involved, they will tend to make the decision that favors the relationship over the one that benefits the business. After all, the family members have to face each other every night across the dinner table.

Second, it is difficult, if not impossible, to fire a non-performing employee or founder, when that employee is your spouse, child, parent or in-law. And if you do fire them, think about the interaction at the next family gathering.

Third, when there are family members in a company, getting the tag of nepotism is easy. It sends a signal to employees that to get ahead or be heard, you need to be 'part of the family'. Everyone else is naturally 'out of the circle' and has a glass ceiling over his/her progression within the company.

Fourth, if you combine the above two points, it becomes demoralizing to employees who see that a non-performing employee/founder can get away with doing sub-par work. They then strive for the same sub-par level, and the competent ones leave.

Though conventional wisdom holds that investing in a firm with family members is fraught with challenges, we ended up investing in Bengaluru-based Openbank, one of the most successful companies I have been involved with.

The team has four solid co-founders, led by Anish Achuthan as the CEO and Deena Jacob, COO/ CFO. The other two co-founders are Anish's wife Mabel Chacko who heads marketing and his brother Ajeesh who heads the technology. I have observed them closely, as Unicorn India Ventures was their first institutional investor, and I have been on the board now for four years. They have a thorough professional relationship among themselves and do not let personal relationships impair the decision-making in any which way. It clearly shows that founders need a different level of maturity to be able to handle these situations. And I am glad that we broke our own unwritten rule of not investing in family related founders and invested in Openbank.

Having a complementary and compatible spouse does not mean you will raise a good, successful, and happy child, but it does increase the chances. So, also is the case co-founders and start-ups.

BEING START-UP BATTLE READY

- Choosing the right co-founder lays the core foundation of the start-up.
- Ensure your co-founder has the same vision and motivations for the entrepreneurial journey.
- Complementarity in skill-sets and emotional makeup is key to a successful relationship.
- There needs to a clear 'first among equals' within the co-founders.
- Having family members as co-founders, usually, further complicates the relationship.
- Have formal legal documentation between co-founders covering all aspects including breakups.

5

RAISING THE FIRST FUNDING ISN'T THE DESTINATION, IT IS THE START OF THE JOURNEY

Every founder goes through the dilemma of 'to raise or not to raise funds'. There are several examples in the industry where founders have chosen not to raise external funds and have still managed to do well, and there are businesses which have raised enormous amounts of funds to scale faster.

I admire Rajesh Jain for several of his qualities as an entrepreneur but the one thing that I really appreciate is his firm belief and focus in not raising any external funding to build his entrepreneurial successes. Both his entrepreneurial stints, IndiaWorld, a B2C-focused news portal that he successfully sold to Sify in 1998, and Netcore, his current business, are self-funded and grew organically.

'It is not that I never approached VCs for funds. Even during IndiaWorld, we had reached out to investors. But I knew the valuation of my company and I told the investor the same, and I never compromised on it. I always focused on making the business profitable. Once you are profitable, there is no pressure to meet external capital to meet payroll requirements,' said Rajesh when I asked him how he managed to build his business without external funding.

Manoj Kanumuri founder of Zen3, an AI-first data-driven and cloud-native business which he recently sold to Tech Mahindra, is another such person I know. He never raised any money from investors. He started with consulting services and ploughed back the cash generated into creating two product platforms based on AI.

Says Manoj, 'Instead of raising money from investors I made sure that the cash-generating business is used for creating a new value-proposition for the company. It was not a conscious decision to not tap into the VC ecosystem. We did take working capital loans from banks. It's just that we didn't feel the need to tap into VC money. I do feel that this business model is best suited for a B2B services business. B2C is a scale business and to be able to compete in the market you need to invest upfront.'

CAPITAL MATTERS

With a thriving start-up ecosystem in the country, founders today have much better access to funds than a decade ago. I am often asked by entrepreneurs about the different cycles of funding for a venture.

While there are no hard and fast definitions, in my view, the funding paths of a start-up can be defined as self-funding/bootstrapping, friends and family funding, seed stage, early-stage, expansion stages, mezzanine-pre-IPO leading onto an exit or an IPO.

Self-funding/bootstrapping is the first phase of the investment stages, when the founders invest their money to begin the start-up journey. On an average, I typically see that a founder has contributed at least ₹10 lakh to their idea before going to the next stage of investment. However, if you are a second-time entrepreneur or someone who has had a long professional career with high salary, you should be expected to put in at least ₹50 lakhs and above. It is important for a founder to have 'skin in the game' if they plan on raising money from investors later. For this reason, it is important to have this round and keep it well documented, so the money put in by the investor is clearly shown as equity in the balance sheet.

During the **friends and family phase** of investing, you are reaching out to people close to you and asking them to put a portion of their life savings in your idea. Be careful. Many founders have burned bridges as they raised money from friends and family. Some of the common mistakes founders commit in this phase are to sell too much equity or sell the wrong kind of equity. Typically, this is the first external round of funding being raised by the founder and the size is around ₹1–2 crore.

We shall talk of this in detail, later in the chapter.

The seed stage of investing is the first phase of raising institutional capital. Usually, this round is sourced from professionals, angel investors, either individually or in an angel group. In most cases, angel investors were or still are founders of companies. Since angels have experience being a previous founder of a business, they can provide more than just capital. You should look for three things in an angel investor: wisdom (done it before), wealth (can help you in future rounds) and the will to work (make sales intros, spend time and be your bouncing board). This round generally allows one to raise around ₹2–5 crore.

Early-stage investing is your first round of venture capital. Usually, this begins and ends with a Series A. During this stage, you should expect to have a much more formal board, and your leadership team becomes more 'professionalized'. Professionalization is a fancy word that means that your buddy, whom you hired as VP, could get fired and be replaced with a seasoned executive. A classic Series A raises between ₹20–40 crore. If you made it to the expansion phase, which is post-Series A and into later rounds (Series B onwards), you have done well.

Very few companies make it to this stage. The **expansion stage** is where you are growing month over month. You have proven that you can scale your business. Valuations and committed capital vary wildly in this phase and are heavily negotiated. Your chances of survival are much higher, and you are on the path of success and achieving your dreams. However, the markets can change any time, especially in technology businesses, and you can easily become an acquisition target by a larger player in the same segment.

The mezzanine or pre-IPO round is the final raise before going public. In the mezzanine round, a company is valued over several hundred million. At this point, the company has hundreds of employees and is operating in more than one country. The company is starting to speak with investment banks, and the leadership team is working on filing documentation. Usually, if you were an early investor, you have been waiting for over 10 years to get to this stage and are more than ready to have a liquidity event—in this case, an IPO. As an angel investor and founder I think it is advisable to sell out before reaching this stage, unless, very early on, you realize that the company will be a unicorn, and assiduously work on to keep your stake in the business.

BANKING ON FAMILY AND FRIENDS

In India, from 2014 to 2019, about 8,900–9,000 start-ups have been incepted, an overall base growing at 12–15 per cent year-on-year, as per Nasscom-Zinnov: Indian Tech Start-up Ecosystem[6]. The total funding received by start-ups in 2019 (Jan–Sep) was \$4.4 billion.

According to a Reserve Bank of India survey on start-ups, families and friends emerged as the primary source of funding. Of the 1,246 start-ups surveyed between November 2018 and April 2019, nearly 43 per cent of respondents said that families and friends were the largest source of funding, apart from own funds[7].

Early investors don't bet on ideas but on you, the founder. The first money you will raise especially if you are a first-time entrepreneur will be most likely from friends and family. The chance of your idea being a success is slim. Without a track-record, it would be difficult to convince an unknown investor to back you. Friends and family on the other hand, are the people who know you, trust you and believe in you. Make no mistakes—they aren't backing your idea but backing you.

Raising any amount of money is a challenge and huge responsibility but this becomes fraught with complications when you raise it from friends and family. The start-up world is replete with unfortunate horror stories of friendships and families broken over bad investments. However, there are stories which are the anti-theses of this as well.

At the Fund, we were considering making an investment in an e-gaming company based out of Ahmedabad. Soham Thacker was a dynamic founder in his early 30s who was starting a gaming platform, GamerJi. He was a second-time entrepreneur and had earlier started a

---

[6]'Nasscom-Zinnov Study, 2019' *Start-up India*. www.startupindia.gov.in/content/sih/en/reources/market-research.html. Accessed 21 November 2020.

[7]'Pilot Survey on Indian Start-up Sector.' *Reserve Bank of India - Reports*, www.rbi.org.in/Scripts/PublicationReportDetails.aspx?UrlPage=&ID=956#46. Accessed 21 November 2020.

web-based business which he shut after three years. He had an angel investor who had funded his earlier venture and upon closure of that business had lost the money. Yet, when we were doing the due diligence, I discovered that the same investor had again backed him in his second venture, GamerJi. Upon speaking to the investor, we realized that despite losing the capital, he had no regrets and felt that Soham did all he could to keep the business afloat and that it was in everyone's best interest to shut the business. Being an astute investor, he decided to back Soham again, as he felt that he would have gained from his previous failure. For us, as potential investors, this was the ultimate ratification of the entrepreneur.

If you have friends and family who will back your start-up, consider yourself fortunate. But be clear to them about the risks of the same. Explain to them the risk in detail. Unlike professional VCs, who should be left to find the risks, to friends and family you must be upfront. Explain to them that in this asset class, most fail and while you will do everything possible to do justice to their faith and investments, nothing is guaranteed.

One of the entrepreneurs whom I admire for balancing his personal relations when he raised money from family and friends is Saumil Majmudar of SportzVillage. He agrees that raising money from family can be tricky. 'I did a few things. I decided that when it came to valuation, if the valuation was 100, I would give it for 90. So, my conscience is clear that I gave you the best deal. People also invest because of trust. They see that the company is moving, that it's growing and overall, their value is increasing. This model of taking small amounts of money from family and friends also worked for us as it helped us on our timeline. If we had taken large sums from a few individuals, we would not have been able to extend the timeline so much and would have been forced to take decisions so that we could return the money faster,' said Saumil.

Only raise money from those who can afford to lose that capital. This is the most vital rule. Often, friends and family, either out of emotional attachment or thinking it could be a jackpot, put in more capital than they should and when they lose big, the relationship is marred forever.

Keep deal structures simple and despite it being a close relationship, employ lawyers to draft legal documentation. This is essential. Often during friends and family rounds, entrepreneurs try to avoid paying legal costs but it comes to haunt them later. And most importantly, you must be aware of what you are entering into and what having an outside investor means.

NO SAFETY NET

Entrepreneurs often ask me, 'When should we quit the job and can we not raise funds from friends and family and then quit, so there is some safety net?'

Often executives try to moonlight their start-up. While in the initial days it might suffice, once the idea is in fruition and the MVP has been rolled out, you ought to take a leap of faith. If you don't believe your idea will succeed, how can you convince any investor of the same? And how will anyone else believe in you. Without you, the entrepreneur, taking the risk, how can you attract team members, customers and investors? It is true that you start with nothing, but you do have your determination, skills and ability.

An incident is etched in my mind. I had a meeting with Sunil (name changed). He was a middle-level executive with a large insurance company. He had a stellar background and deep domain expertise in insurance. He had clearly seen a market deficiency and had brainstormed a plan for an insurtech business which was looking at making the onboarding, risk management and premium calculation process seamless for customers. The model was something of interest to Unicorn India Ventures, as we believed the insurance industry globally, but particularly in India, was rife for digital transformation. We were keen to back the business.

However, he had a deep fear of the unknown and was ensconced in his job and unwilling to take the plunge. For over six months, he would meet the time and seek affirmation on the business model but was unwilling to take the plunge. He was looking at us to fund the business before quitting his job. This was a no-go for us. If he was hesitant to take the risk and show faith in his own plan, how could any investor back him. In hindsight, we are glad that early on itself, we came to know of this character trait. Putting head above parapet and taking the risk is the foremost attribute of an entrepreneur, which Sunil lacked, though he was a successful executive.

The early rounds of friends/family and angel investors are the first exposure of the entrepreneur to fundraising. Any successful entrepreneur will spend the rest of his life in the fundraise mode and in talking to investors. Investor meetings require a skill-set different from operations or coding. All successful entrepreneurs must adapt themselves to handle this aspect during their entrepreneurial journey. This is something which cannot be delegated to external advisors and CFOs even for listed businesses. Investors want to look entrepreneurs in the eye before they sign a cheque.

In India, there are now quite a few angel platforms. Besides this, there are active angels who have made substantial returns over the last decade. The angel network has strongly emerged in India over the last decade and has been a driver for the start-up ecosystem. The basic tool-kit for raising angel funding is a clearly articulated elevator pitch for the business, a pitch deck, a MVP (or at least a working prototype) and early adapters or customers.

Often, entrepreneurs ask me about the key attributes that angel investors look at. I put this question to Kishore Ganji, a prolific angel investor who has built a portfolio of over 50 businesses across India and the US.

According to Kishore, the key drivers that he looks for are:

- The quality, passion, commitment and integrity of the founders.
- The market opportunity being addressed and the potential for the company to become big.
- A clearly thought-out business plan, and any early evidence of obtaining traction towards the plan.
- Interesting technology or intellectual property.
- Appropriate valuation with reasonable terms.
- The viability of raising additional rounds of financing if progress is made.

A mentor is also extremely important when it comes to understanding and selecting investors. Sanjay Anandaram, who has been mentor and advisor to several start-ups says, 'Having mentors on board helps as they can point out if there is a DNA mismatch between the founder, investors and the board member. Mentors help founders understand investors, guide the founder in selecting the appropriate investors and team members, and advise them on managing investors and any conflicts.'

ANGELS AND DEMONS

As a founder, closing an angel investment is the first hurdle in the steeplechase of entrepreneurial life that you are looking to cross. You are naturally circumspect, tense and desperate to close the round, and move on. But you need to be aware of the type of angel to go with. Once the round is closed, you will need to co-exist with these angel investors. There are a several examples of companies that are unable to scale up because of the wrong types of angels.

Entrepreneurs need to be aware of 'real' angel investors. The world is fraught with folks who pretend to be angel investors but are not actually so—they look for start-ups that they can jump on board with, either as an employee or consultant. There is another class of angel investor who are the unscrupulous types. They will come across as if they have a pile of cash to invest and will offer to put together a half-million-dollar round for you, of which they will commit substantial capital of their own! So far, so good. However, once the round starts coming together, they start backing off their personal investment (usually all the way down to zero) and instead ride the momentum into a job. Instead of investing, they will pitch for an advisory role, and will take a bunch of equity to boot.

Then there are angel investors who drive a hard bargain. They will put in substantial capital and spark the round for you. But they will ultimately want about 75 per cent of the company to do it. These are new to angel investment business and think that driving a hard bargain is the name of the game. They do not realize that by doing so, they will kill the company and your motivation to be an entrepreneur.

Then there are those who had no intention ever to invest but will take you down the garden path asking due diligence questions and waste your time, in the hope that you see the value they bring to them and offer them some free equity.

As an entrepreneur you need to have the guts to ask some of the prospective angel investors some serious questions. Such as, how long the person has been an investor, check with known reputable angel investors and local venture capitalists on both the person and the companies they have been involved in to get a sense of how 'real' the prospective investor is, research their background and find out if they are likely to have the type of liquidity necessary to make angel investments.

None of these questions or tactics will be offensive to real angel investors. In fact, they will give the real ones more confidence in you. These tactics might offend the fake ones, driving them away.

The hunt for the angel round is time consuming and could take up to six months to a year. It is all-subsuming and draws the time, energy and effort of the entrepreneur. This is in addition to running and growing the business, as during the times of funding, the business needs to show growth and positive metrics.

Founders are up to the brim with stress, anxiety and exhaustion as they come to the closure of the angel rounds. But they cannot afford any short-cuts. They need to remember that closing the angel round is an important milestone in the journey, but not the destination.

TRACK RECORD MATTERS

Not all founding teams have to through this journey of raising funds. Second-time established entrepreneurs with credibility and a proven track-record start at a different level. Of late, there have been several second-time founders who have started their business with enough capital to back them. Founders like Kunal Shah, Mukesh Bansal and Jiten Gupta with their successful first exits raised capital even before their product was established.

One such co-founder is Amod Malviya of Udaan, 'I do not talk much about the investor interest in us at a very early-stage because I think people will not understand the nuances. We left Flipkart after a massive success, so we were carrying a significant advantage. The team that came together for Udaan was the one that built Flipkart.' He said, when investors look at investment, they see one of these three things: one, either the investor believes in the idea very strongly and sees you to be the best person/

team to solve it. Two, the investor does not know about the area much, but you are able to create a product that can demonstrate it is solving a big problem (product-market fit). And three, you have a great team the investors are confident about.

'We raised our first round of funding even before our product was launched, so I think we would fall in the third bucket. Without having the background that we have had because of Flipkart, this would not have happened. Of course, the fact that we had put in substantial capital in Udaan also helped. Our thought process was that we are looking to solve the B2B e-commerce problem in a different form than the B2C format, but what the format was—we were not sure. So, we decided to put in money and we had decided that once we formed the product-market fit we will raise funds. When we started talking to investors, we were not looking to raise, but what gave them confidence was also the fact that we had our skin in the game. And that is hugely respected by investors. Later, investment was based on the fact that we could see a quick product-market fit and rapid scale out,' shared Amod.

BEING START-UP BATTLE READY

- You have to take the risk before any investor backs you.
- Initial investors bet on the entrepreneur and not on the idea or the business.
- Take money from those friends and family who can afford it, but be upfront with the caveats.
- Be totally prepared when going for fundraising, as you have only one chance.
- Be aware of certain types of angels and be prepared to ask them questions.
- Understand all the nuances of negotiations and take legal advice for all documentation.

6

VISION DOES NOT ENSURE SUCCESS, EXECUTION DOES

Whenever a story is written or a film made about the success of a start-up founder, the eye-catching headline is always about the 'eureka moment', the struggle to get the first funding, the founder's strife with co-founders and investors and the big bang exit or IPO.

What most storytellers gloss over are the central and most painstaking parts of the journey: the daily execution with its challenges and the pains of scaling up. Daily execution entails the nitty gritty work of product prioritization, decisions regarding customer segmentation and the customer feedback to re-work on the product, constantly challenging the numbers and testing for better results. This of course, is in addition to managing daily cash-flows and building the team. These do not provide for an interesting script and are often neglected by writers of history; but it is this razor-focused execution that makes for a scalable business.

Thus far, the founders have depended on their gut and intuition but as they scale, they now need to shift gears and their decisions need to be driven by data. To be able to inculcate this, requires a change in personality of the founders. The good news is that doing so is the first step towards the making of a leader of a scale-up.

UNDERSTAND START-UP BUSINESS METRICS

After having raised initial capital and launched the MVP, the founder must shift gears and focus on the daily operational grime. His focus must now be to lay the foundations of the business growth.

A lot of founders are good at selling the big picture of the vision, but cannot adjust to this change and cannot scale the business. One of the key drivers in this phase of growth and which isn't highlighted in the success or failure stories is the 'definition of the business metrics'—understanding the true financial numbers and constantly analyzing them with the honesty. One should also be aware that the metrics of your business keeps changing as the business evolves.

Accounting, as a function in large and traditional enterprises, is seen as monotonous and boring. They are a tool in the hands of the CEO and the board to hold each divisional manager 'accountable' in reaching their goals and the sum of the performances makes up the performance of the enterprise. Not so in a start-up. Given the nature of start-ups, these aren't the measurements to gauge the performance of the entrepreneur. Start-ups, by definition, are unpredictable for traditional accounting practices of milestones, forecasts and measurements.

In a start-up, the accounting function must be integral to the business and should be driven by the founder. This is the business accounting which is the key vis-a-vis the financial reporting.

In a classical manufacturing business, the growth is in proportion to sales. The gross margin of the business is invested into sales and marketing for enhancing the sales and the bottom-line. Newer capital investments are made to add newer machinery and lines to increase capacity to add new variants which will deepen the customer relationship and hence, improve yield per customer or open newer markets for customers. This is simplistically the essence of a manufacturing business. Compare this with the online business models, these businesses need a different set of metrics.

First and foremost, a start-up needs to define the metrics such that within the company and among the investors, the understanding of the nomenclature is the same. This might sound incredulous, but in almost every Board Meeting I sit on, irrespective of the size of the business, considerable time is spent in understanding the terminology, so that all participants are on the same page.

Some of the terms most founders are familiar with which need clear articulation or else leads to confusion among stakeholders are bookings vs revenues, total revenue vs recurring revenue, total contract value vs annual contract value, gross margins vs net margins, gross merchandise value (GMV) vs revenues, deferred revenues vs billings, and signups vs active users.

According to Anil Joshi, managing partner of Unicorn India Ventures, who has made early-stage investment in over 100 businesses, 'While for the industry, these definitions are more or less clear, it is best that each company customizes them in relevance to their business. The same needs to be circulated right across to the start-up team and the other stakeholders, like advisors, auditors and of course, the investors.'

In offline businesses, you meet customers physically. They are either buying your manufactured product or are entering the retail store to buy what you have displayed. They are customers at your restaurant or walking into a movie theatre to watch a film. Over decades, we are all aware of the traditional marketing methods to know the customer better.

In online businesses, companies need to understand the consumer as well as they would an offline customer, if not better. They need to understand the most important matrix which makes and breaks a lot of online businesses—the customer acquisition costs (CAC). Once you have the customers, it is important to retain them. Often businesses are obsessed with gaining new customers and neglect existing customers.

You need to keep innovating your retention schemes in order to reduce the dangerous 'churn rate'. When I used to head a pay television business in the late 1990s, the cost of getting a new customer was 5–6 times that of retaining a customer. The most controversial of all customer metrics is 'the lifetime value (LTV) of customer'. The holy grail of digital businesses is the LTV and it should be higher than the CAC. The larger the difference, the greater are the chances of success of the company.

In order to increase the LTV of customers, businesses like Amazon and Flipkart are constantly adding new service offerings to get a 'greater share of the wallet' spend of the customer.

While this sounds plain vanilla, for a start-up, implementing these effectively is the challenge the founder is constantly grappling with. The triangulation of getting data from the business, making rapid changes based on the data and implementing the same repeatedly towards a positive upward spiral is the path to success for businesses.

One company I have been involved with, which has accomplished this is SmartCoin, a digital lending company which provides micro-loans of ₹1,000–₹5,000 to consumers for a month. Typically, their customers are blue-collared folk who do have regular income, but are not considered eligible for loans by traditional financial institutions.

When Unicorn India Ventures invested in the company, the team of four founders had built the MVP, tested their product and used their own capital of ₹20–25 lakh. We have been invested with the company for over four years and have seen the company scale up and raise substantial capital from international investors, and are now lending close to ₹50 crore per month.

The technology platform was the underpinning of their entire business model and they catered to a large loan book and approximately gave 5,000 loans a day with a team of only 70 odd staff. Compare this with any traditional micro-finance company that would have well over 500 people to cater to such a loan book with similar default rates.

The way the company had scaled up with the right metrics was extremely pleasing to both Anil and me. I firmly believe their blueprint should be followed by all B2C digital companies. They were very conscious of their CACs and they strongly believed, from the first instance, in customer retention. Their retention rate, defined by returning customers for loan, was as high as 80 per cent. They realized that for a business giving loans, it is easy to have vanity metrics of scaling up as everyone wants a loan. They would, however, always keep a close watch on the delinquency rate (the default rate of customers not paying back).

Classical product development cycles talk about defining the base level. Once you have the base level defined, you innovate on the product and re-launch the next version to see the improvements and scale up. After some time, again you take the feedback loop and get back to the next sprint. And you analyze the performance of each cohorts between the sprints.

This is exactly what SmartCoin did as they constantly worked on their credit and ratings engine, which was the secret sauce of the business. They would scale up the lending and test the credit engine. Once it crossed the threshold level set for defaults, they would freeze the lending levels, re-work on the credit engine and relaunch the next version and start lending again.

Says Rohit Garg, founder and CEO of the business, 'We would spend time in analyzing each cohort and study the improvements from the previous cycle across various business parameters. It is because of this sprint cycle of product development that we scaled up 1,000 times of lending in four years without increasing the single most important determinant of business "the default rate".'

VANITY METRICS

Understanding the relevance of metrics is as important as the metric itself. In the start-up world, we have a term called 'vanity metrics'. Many founders, especially those who have raised some funding, go overboard to impress their investors and create a 'media buzz' in the market. Without their knowledge and without a malintent heart, they resort to shoring up the vanity metrics.

Helping focus the founders towards meaningful metrics which are actionable and in sync with the business goals is a duty of the investors and advisors. One such example is Inc42, India's foremost start-up media company and of which I am a Board Director.

The young team of founders—Vaibhav Vardhan, Utkarsh Agarwal and Pooja Sareen—are extremely passionate about the business and were building a 'great brand' but not a 'great business'. The founders thought they were doing the right thing because their registered users, active users and page views were growing. Their revenues too were growing. Coming from a media background, I realized that they were unknowingly going after the 'vanity metrics' and couldn't tell the difference between that and the actionable metrics.

I introduced Shantanu Bhanja, former CEO of HT Digital (part of the listed Hindustan Times Group) and a close friend of mine, to Inc42's board as an advisor and investor in the business. Says Shantanu, 'Inc42 had clearly managed to establish a brand and a reputation in the start-up community. What they needed to build was the rigour of driving an unwavering focus throughout the organization—from every person on the editorial team to marketing and sales—on consistently and single-mindedly recruiting new users through driving discoverability of content, stickiness, page views/session and time on page, and tracking engagement across all platforms, be it on the site or on social media, or traffic from newsletters.'

Once the whole organization was focused on measuring and driving this, to the exclusion of everything else, the whole energy and rhythm of the organization transformed.

There are hundreds of companies that fail after raising the initial capital. This is not because the ideas were flaky, but because their executions were flawed. Founders want to run; they do not like their enthusiasm to be curbed by data. That is why, having complementary skill-sets amongst co-founders is key, with at least one co-founder always focused on data.

For scaleups to go to the next level, it is essential that founders imbibe data as a core aspect of the DNA of the organization. This must be shared with all employees. Founders may, out of sense of insecurity and fear of accepting failure, keep the data to themselves and not share the same with the operating managers in marketing, sales and operations. This defeats the very purpose of data.

Abhinay Choudhari of BigBasket elaborates on metrics and how the company had devised three to four metrics to be measured on a daily basis, as they were scaling up. 'In the online business, the metrics are readily available to be measured. We are always in touch with the pulse of the business. We have three to four key metrics—on-time delivery, out of stock, fill rates and customer complaints. These metrics had to be churned out every day, and you know what is working or not working, and are immediately able to take decisions. This helped the teams immensely,' said Abhinay.

BEING START-UP BATTLE READY

- Numbers don't lie; respect data and build the business based around data.
- Define the metrics that define the success factor for your start-up, and articulate the same to the team and investors.
- As you generate data, be sure to work in small sample sets and undertake cohort analysis.
- Chase metrics that matter to the sustainability of the business and not vanity metrics for ego or media coverage.
- To align the management team, the founder must not be afraid to share the data.
- The management team must work towards improving the actionable metrics.

7

THEY NEED TO KNOW YOU BUILT IT, FOR THEM TO COME TO IT

EVERY FOUNDER IS A SALESMAN

The best salesperson, in my opinion, was Steve Jobs. Many feel that his death created a vacuum in the technology world; he was a marketing genius. He was perhaps the only CEO who had a very close and long relationship with Apple's advertisement agency TBWA\Chiat\Day and would be involved in all product campaigns. His involvement was evident in their product strategy, as his products were always superior, carried an exclusive tag and he made sure they were sold at a premium. Michael Hageloh, a former Apple sales executive and author of *Live from Cupertino: How Apple Used Words, Music, and Performance to Build the World's Greatest Sales Machine*, writes that Steve Jobs's real talent wasn't design—it was seduction; of making one fall in love with the products that Apple made.[8]

Founders need to remember this. Before they create their A-team or hire sales executives, they themselves must be the first to make customers come on board. Founders of well-funded early-stage businesses make the

---

[8]"Steve Jobs's Real Talent Wasn't Design-It Was Seduction." *Fast Company*. www.fastcompany.com/90458207/steve-jobss-real-talent-wasnt-design-it-was-seduction. Accessed 21 November 2020.

classic mistake of hiring a sales team too early and expect it to deliver numbers. This thought forms the core of *Everything Started as Nothing*— you have to build everything from scratch for your business. You will be the company's first salesman, administrator, HR and even technician.

My first venture, Recreate Solutions, received its first round of funding in October 2000, and even before our value proposition was defined, we hired a sales team in the UK comprising of senior folks from a large US digital business. We thought they would come with the Rolodex needed for us to be able to sell the 'India advantage in content conversion business'. Sadly, my co-founder and I hadn't yet made any substantial sale. We were expecting the sales team to do the job for us with their experience, a cardinal mistake.

In less than six months, we had to fire them and while at that time, I had blamed their incompetency, in hindsight, I realized that the fault was entirely mine. As the founder of the business, if I could not close the initial sales and win marquee accounts, how I could expect a newly hired sales team with no idea of my vision or conviction to be able to manage a sales closure?

The Rolodex and contacts matter but defining the market and approach is more important, and that is the job of the founder. I had a wonderful discussion with Phanindra (Phani) Sama, the founder of Redbus, regarding delegation and sales team. Redbus was one of the early success stories of the Indian start-up consumer internet ecosystem. Phani and his co-founders Charan Padmaraju and Sudhakar Pasupunuri were all friends from BITS Pilani and were working in various technology multinationals in Bangalore.

From his experience, Phani has so aptly put it, 'The first pursuit for a founder has to be getting the product-market fit. Rather, I would suggest that until you get the product-market fit, don't even think of delegating. Only after you see some green shoots should you think of hiring any sales team and contemplate delegating. And once the initial sales happen without the founders, then it is time to crank up the sales engine.'

Sales is the lifeline of any business and in the case of start-ups, it is no different. Founders need to fundamentally be sales guys. They need to be selling, even when they are not selling to customers. Most of the time, the founders are either selling their vision to team members or potential hires, or they are convincing investors to buy their story and, these days, also selling their dream idea to media outlets to write about them.

CRANKING UP SALES

In high technology companies, especially where the founders are part of the product development team, they believe that if the product is good, customers will flock to it. They view their own jobs as intellectual, rooted to their laptops and working hard at coding. Whereas when they see the sales team, whom they view as having lower intellect, on long lunches with clients and laughing with their customers, they often feel the people in sales have all the fun and yet are unable to sell the 'fruits of their labour'.

Most tech people lobby to the CEO that their product is perfect, and it is the fault of the 'sales guys' for not being able to sell. This is far from the truth. In fact, sometimes the converse is true that great products do not sell because the founders have not defined how to promote and distribute the product.

How do you acquire new customers? For companies which are in direct acquisitions, these are driven by two growth drivers: paid and viral. These have been discussed at length by the pundits, especially for SaaS business (software-as-service). I thought I would draw some simple illustrations for new founders.

Paid engine of growth is when the start-up, after having established the product-market fit, is ready to crank up the sales engine. They employ various modes of reaching the customers, which include digital outreach. Let us assume the monthly spend over various digital media is ₹500,000 and the SaaS business acquires 500 clients, its cost per acquisition (CPA) is ₹1000. Now, if the customer pays ₹100 and typically stays for six months, the company will earn ₹600 from each customer. The business would, therefore, make a gross margin loss per customer.

Most consumer businesses do not have these numbers worked out and while the team is happy they are growing, they are actually losing more and more money. It, therefore, becomes imperative that these businesses are well funded and can grow on the back of losses as they operate in segments which are classically defined as 'winner takes all'. Therefore, in this type of industry, there is no position of survival for the third player onwards and only one or two players can survive.

As an investor, I have been through the cycle. In Unicorn India Ventures, we had invested in a business called GrabonRent. They had created a platform to provide online rentals for white goods and furniture. The business was growing but under the onslaught of better funded players, their cost of acquisition went up, as keyword searches, advertising and discounts became expensive. Although the business had better gross margins than its competitors, it fell prey to the 'winner takes all' nature of the industry.

That is why unit metrics are very important for businesses and at the unit-level need to break-even at the earliest. Digital start-ups also need to be aware of how they can leverage their unit losses with other revenues, by being able to monetize their data or advertising. The first step for survival for digital consumer businesses is to reach unit-level break-even.

VIRALITY FACTOR

With the increase of social media and constant interactions, the virality of a product has become a benchmark for growth.

In the recent past, we have seen how various news items and memes have gone viral across different social media. In India, we are used to getting the same meme within minutes from different chat forums. That establishes the virality of the news.

For instance, in the days of COVID, people were aware of the R factor (the reproduction factor). It was known that if R was greater than 1, it meant that the virus would spread to more than one person and the fight for 'flattening the curve' was to reduce the R factor to less than 1. Similarly, for viral marketers, the goal is to drive the V factor (virality factor) to greater than 1. If your V factor is 3, it means that for every person using your product, they are attracting interest from three other persons.

Similarly, when your product goes viral, the cost of distribution is low, your brand awareness grows much faster than you would imagine and there is the instant establishment of credibility. It is the dream of every product owner when their product goes viral.

While there are no established formulae, according to Anil Nair, founder and former CEO, L&K Saatchi & Saatchi, the leading digital media company, 'Some of the good practices of brands who wish their products to go viral are meticulous planning, gamification of the idea and knowing your audience well.' He further adds that one should leverage the ecosystems used by your audience and make sharing natural and easy.

However, in the crowded world of today's internet where every brand and every piece of news is looking at going viral, getting a viral engine of growth is often a pipe dream of product owners.

Students of digital marketing are aware of how Facebook went viral after Zuckerberg launched it in the dorms of Harvard. The other example of virality was the case of Hotmail. After Sabeer Bhatia launched the business, the company wasn't having a great run till they began mentioning 'PS: Get your free email at Hotmail' below every email. With that, every user who got an email from a Hotmail user, starting clicking on the link and opened Hotmail accounts. The numbers went through the roof and within 18 months of launch, the company reached 12 million subscribers and was eventually acquired by Microsoft for $400 million.

COMMUNICATION IS ESSENTIAL

Often after closing a large funding round, digital businesses go into print and television advertising. I have a personal view on the relevance of offline traditional advertising with traditional brands.

Every entrepreneur and investor pines for a recognizable advertising campaign on primetime television. But start-ups should resist the temptation to fight the bigger and traditional businesses for memorable television spots. Traditional companies take years of funding to be able to have a distribution channel and offering for masses that would justify spending on television and mainstream press. When digital businesses, suddenly flush with venture funding, start advertising in mainstream media, it leads to a lot of wastage.

Only much later in their lifecycle of growth should start-ups consider mainstream outlets. It is also interesting to note that most start-ups have strong metrics around digital advertising but given the opacity of performance metrics in traditional advertising, they are unable to control the spends, unlike traditional companies who have built years of knowledge on the same. It is because of this, India is replete of stories of start-ups blowing up investor equity on television, print and other traditional media and going bust.

The story of Housing.com's ₹120 crore marketing campaign is well known. The campaign was to utilize print, out-of-home (billboards and hoardings) and digital media to create impact and was expected to spread over three phases, over a time-frame of eight weeks. At the time, the founders had defended their decision to run such an expensive campaign on the grounds that the traffic to the website had increased 500 per cent since the launch of the campaign.

What happened after that is well documented, but the key lesson here is that the game changer of this campaign would have been a shift from vanity metrics to true business fundamentals. Also, investors today have matured and are not taken in by advertising for future rounds of funding. So, founders should really consider long and hard before embarking on highly expensive traditional brand advertising.

However, the same is not true for PR and social media. In the present day crowded market, start-ups need to be heard. And working closely with relevant media through innovative means and using social media for talking to all stakeholders is absolutely essential for every start-up founder. This is something which we tell every start-up founder, especially those who are product facing and who believe PR and social media is all fluff. What they don't realize is that communication is essential not only for their customers, but for their present employees, for attracting future talent, for competition and for future investors.

THE GUMPTION TO WIN

The driver and model for enterprise sales is different. India is replete with success stories of Information Technology (IT) businesses where the companies started with small sales and now these single sales orders are multi-billion dollars spread across multiple years. Compared to the glamorous digital business of today, IT services is looked upon as boring and staid business; but it is this IT services that has transformed India in terms of global image, employment generation and the creation of a large aspirational middle class. Each of these players has painstakingly worked on their branding and PR to create a global image.

Infosys, in many ways, is India's first true start-up. The lore of Infosys is well known to most Indians: started in 1981, by seven founders who were friends and colleagues, with a meager $250, it has become a behemoth of revenues of over $12 billion and market cap in excess of $53 billion[9].

Though not a founder in the company, one of the key drivers in the growth of Infosys, from being a $1 million company when he joined it, to one with a revenue of $750 million when he left it is, Phaneesh Murthy.

I was fortunate to have a long chat with Phaneesh on the various aspects of growing the business, the early entrepreneurial instinct for sales and how he built the sales organization in an industry that didn't exist. There are deep learnings to take from what Phaneesh and his motley crew did in the '90s, which are lessons for any enterprise sales teams.

Says Phaneesh, 'I started out in 1992 and came to the US. I started the whole process from scratch and got into the building of a business in the US. Got some very lucky breaks. Getting into deals was also quite interesting then. I remember losing out on a deal because that company called the Indian Embassy in San Francisco asking for companies that they could work with for software solutions—they were told about Tata and Wipro. I again lost another deal because a customer called up the US Embassy in India asking for software companies that they could work with. This made me realize that at some point of time we will need to get into branding, because addressing such people was like getting caught in a spider's web.'

Phaneesh created a branding proposition that was based on the idea of a 'lotus blooming in a marsh'. 'The idea, then, was in a country where

[9]"Infosys FY20 revenues.' *Infosys*. https://www.infosys.com/investors/reports-filings/quarterly-results/2019-2020/q4/documents/ifrs-usd-press-release.pdf. Accessed 21 November 2020.

businesses were not being run transparently, here is a company which is going to be extremely transparent and honest in its accounting, will be releasing results soon and on time, in different GAAP (generally accepted accounting principles) and will be slicing and dicing the data and making it simpler for the shareholders and the markets to understand. The branding also reflected on the key spokespersons, N.R.N. Murthy's, values. The process was very rewarding, because we were a part of a company in the making, an industry in the making and a country in the making,' shared Phaneesh. And the rest, as they say, is history.

While Phaneesh's story of creating a brand for a growing organization will no doubt serve as a beacon for all those looking to build an enterprise, this is not the only way to grow an enterprise sales company.

Manoj Kanumuri was a senior director with Microsoft when he left to start his own business, Zen3 Infosolutions. He built a company which leveraged AI and focused on creating solutions based on Microsoft's platform. Instead of going wide, he was able to develop the relationship with a single client, Microsoft. This was a strategy fraught with risk as his client concentration was nearly 70 per cent with one client. But Manoj was sure of the value-add that it brought to the table.

Says Manoj, 'Along with developing new clients, we kept deepening our client relationship with Microsoft. Our tech team knew the Microsoft product set around Azure very well. We provided Microsoft the flexibility and speed which the larger players could not give. To further deepen the relationship, we had made an acquisition in the US of a company which also provided other services within Microsoft. While we had competition as this is a generic area, we build our competency centre around AI annotation space.'

In March 2020, Zen3 got acquired by Tech Mahindra within six years of starting, and Manoj now heads the Microsoft practice. His story is different from that of the other IT services players, as he built the business on the back of a single client and single expertise—but built scale to become attractive for a buyer.

EVERYONE IS 'NOT' YOUR TARGET MARKET

Often during start-up pitches, I have heard founders say, 'Everyone is in our target market'. This phrase is as off-putting for an investor as hearing 'I have no competition,' as discussed in the earlier chapter.

One can understand that founders feel that by defining their target market, they maybe restricting their scope and feel ill at ease to proclaim to the world, 'This is who we are.' But saying everyone is their target market, just means that their product does not appeal to anyone in particular. Hence, the key is to define the markets that you are after and the customer problem that you are solving.

In simple terms, a target market is a group or groups of consumers/ clients for whom the product/service is intended. Founders need to remember that by defining the target audience, one is not putting a ceiling on how high your company can fly. Defining the target market solves problems around the start-up spectrum, from product design and development to market development and messaging.

Honing in on a specific target market does a few things for a start-up:

1. Brings focus to the product: The success of a start-up depends on having a plan that revolves around having a product/service that directly addresses a pain point of the target. The more well-defined your target market, the clearer your understanding of the problem statement and therein, the better you can calibrate the product to solve it.

2. Clarity of messaging: It also brings clarity to your messaging, and how you go about explaining your value to your would-be customers. The more narrowly you define the target market, the more focused you can get with messaging to them.

3. Better value for the cost: Being targeted gives you the means of reaching the audiences with lesser marketing wastage. This makes the marketing dollar go much farther and gives the start-up more runways to establish itself.

Founders should not have to feel that defining target market will narrow their long-term vision of 'world domination'. Companies that today are ubiquitous and spread in all directions, started with narrow, focused target markets. We all know Facebook, which now has almost 3 billion users worldwide, started as a social networking site specifically for students at Mark Zuckerberg's alma mater, Harvard. Then, it expanded to a handful of other colleges. Later, it opened up to anyone with a .edu email address. Finally, they opened Facebook to anyone over the age of 13 with a valid email address, three years after it launched.

Similarly, Flipkart started with books and then expanded to other areas in the electronics segment, phones and developed their unique business model including the 'cash-on-delivery' payment mode, and then increased their market reach by acquiring Myntra and Jabong. When they started expanding, they expanded fast, hitting 35 cities in a matter of months. But still, they started small—thought carefully about who they were going after, every step of the way.

I was struck by Rajat Mohanty's candour in defining the market and how he started. I would also highlight here that are very few Indian entrepreneurs who have chosen the security market and thrived with success.

'It was not that we had already decided upon cyber security. If you remember, this was the time of e-commerce and though the dotcom bust had happened, everybody thought things will move on. We took the analogy of the Gold Rush of 1849, the people who made the money were the ones who were providing services and products related to the Rush, like Levi's, Wells Fargo, etc. Our thought process was that if e-commerce is the next big thing, then what would be the plumbing that could support it. Security looked like a good idea. When we started, nobody talked about security, and today nobody can stop talking about it. We thought if we were early, we could create something different.'

He further added, 'When you are early in an industry segment, the good part is that, though you are learning, you still are ahead of the pack. We started learning everything there was to learn. We got books, attended conferences—whatever could make us aware of this sector, we learnt it. The first year and year-and-a-half was all about learning the tricks of the trade, rather than going into the market.'

◆

As the company builds the sales organization, the focus and drive of the founder changes from inward product focus to a more outward customer focus, as focus shifts towards the front-end of the business. The head of sales or the chief revenue officer becomes the founder's alter-ego, rather than the head of product or head of delivery. The sales organization drives the product. This brings its own challenges, which will be discussed in the next chapter on competition, the constant challenge of keeping the product contemporary and how start-ups need to pivot to remain relevant to their customers.

BEING START-UP BATTLE READY

- Founders need to put on their sales hat; they need to not just sell their products to customers but also their vision to investors, employees, the team around them and their partners.
- Until product-market fit is defined and initial sales are done, only the founder is responsible for the sales.
- For consumer businesses, think through the customer acquisition strategy. It is often easy to get carried away into unprofitable sales which are not sustainable in the long-run.
- Do not advertise for vanity; only do so when the business justifies the same.
- Try for 'virality', though it is difficult in today's crowded market.
- In enterprise sales, define the core sales pitch and build a sales team that can deliver the same.

8

MARKETS ARE EVER-EVOLVING; PIVOT OR PERISH

An important aspect of running a start-up is to realize that change is inevitable. However, to be able to undertake a pivot directly relates to the mindset of the founder.

The market is indeed ever evolving. That is the thrill for founders who enjoy the game of chess in the face of time and competition, and who learn how to pivot their business based on market feedback or systemic environmental changes, and how to react to competition. As Sir Richard Branson has said, 'Successful businesses are the ones that find ways to adapt to change, no matter which direction it comes from.'

The story of the constant pivots in the case of BigBasket is very interesting. When Abhinay Choudhari started the business of ShopasUlike (the earlier avatar of BigBasket), it was a zero-inventory model and he was using the Metro Cash & Carry inventory, their entire back-end, warehouse, etc. and he just took care of the front end. After the creation of BigBasket in 2011, when the company launched its services pan Bangalore, the model was the same. The decision to expand to Mumbai and Hyderabad after raising the Series A fund, was based on the fact that Metro had a presence in these two cities and they wanted to replicate the same model of zero-inventory.

But soon the founders realized the limitation of running the zero-inventory model. They realized that the customer experience was getting compromised and the unit economics of the business was not favourable.

'In the zero-inventory model, since we were using Metro's back-end and warehouse and we were buying from them, they would pocket 8–12 per cent of the margins. This meant we were operating at an 8–9 per cent margin. The second issue was that Metro is a store, which means customers are walking in every day. So, the inventory that I had and based on which a customer had ordered, may not have some items because by the time our team goes to take stuff, the stock is not there. Our fill rate was not good. Metro was giving us, at best, a fill rate of about 80–85 per cent. The other problem was that for whatever was not available at Metro, we would go to Hypermarket and we realized that this was not a model that worked and then we took the call to have our own warehouse.'

After running the business for over a year on the zero-inventory model, BigBasket decided to invest in its own warehouses. The first warehouse was setup in Bangalore in February 2013. After Bangalore, the two other cities—Mumbai and Hyderabad—also moved to this model. While making pivots, one of the cardinal rules that the BigBasket team followed was to always stabilize the new features at one centre and then move to other centres. 'When we moved to this model, there was a huge change at the back end. We first stabilized the three cities we were present in when we moved to the warehouse model. Once these three were running smoothly, we started to expand in other cities,' says Abhinay.

Abhinay believes that pivot is constant in any business. Even today, BigBasket keeps making changes to its business. Recently they merged the Express model with the slotted delivery in Tier 1 cities to offer larger assortment than Express and faster deliveries than slotted delivery. Even as you grow into a successful, big brand, every business decision will be taking you from 'nothing' to 'everything'.

When BigBasket was launched, it was targeted towards the PC user. This meant grocery shopping was a planned and dedicated activity, which would generally be done towards the end of the day on a desktop or laptop. 'The original business plan had assumed that the average customer order size which was then ₹850–900 will go up and it did go up to ₹1,500 but when the apps model came the order size went southwards, as value of each transaction went down but the volumes went up. We had to change a lot of things. Even today, after all the success, we are constantly looking at newer pivots of the business to adapt with the changing times. No business can stay still and handling the pivots is the key driver of the management team,' says Abhinay.

The 'pivot or persevere' dilemma is a fight the founder will have to struggle with throughout their journey. Founders, sometimes, are so attached to the initial idea, having sold it to the team and investors, that they are drowned in their own conviction. They are afraid to acknowledge failure and feel that they need some more time to try the original proposition. There is always a set of team members and also, a set of metrics which will support the original hypothesis. It is here, that the senior folks surrounding the founder—the advisors, investors, board—have a role to play and explain to the founder that only good founders are able to draw on market dynamics and pivot the business.

One of the portfolio companies of Unicorn India Ventures is Pharmarack, a company which is digitizing the broken supply chain of the pharmaceutical industry. Essentially, it was creating a single platform where the pharma companies, distributors and drug stores came together and shared all the data about inventory, order processing and billing. This meant creating a large distribution network of distributors and pharmacies.

We invested in the business in 2016 and for the first two years, the company was rolling out the platform and signing in both distributors and pharmacies onto the platform. However, early on my partner Anil Joshi, who was on the board of the company, realized that while the company was building the platform and scaling it, monetization was a challenge and the company needed a major pivot.

Needless to say, the founders initially resisted the 'pivot' and wanted to 'persevere' with the idea of creating the platform and look at SaaS revenues out of it. Slowly, with logic and rationale, Anil convinced the business that they needed to pivot. Within six months, he roped in a senior gentleman from the pharmaceutical industry as co-founder and CEO of the business, and with his aid, pivoted the business completely. Now, the platform allows pharma supply chain companies to track order management, procurement, returns, collections, market insights and inventory management for the pharmaceutical retailers and distributors.

This pivot has changed the basic paradigm of the business and in less than 18 months, it became a different business, in terms of scale, people and business model.

THERE ARE SMARTER PEOPLE OUT THERE

Having defined the target market and getting the product-market fit, a start-up launches the product. But this isn't a theoretical exercise of an MBA classroom. Often, the market is not what the founder had expected it to be. Even if the market understanding was right, the founders had not realized the difficulty in coming up with the monetization proposition. In such scenarios, it becomes imperative for the founder to pivot the business. Companies that cannot pivot the business to a new direction based on feedback from the marketplace will slowly die, or at best be a living dead.

Take the case of serial entrepreneur Anu Acharya's first start-up Ocimum Biosolutions. Ocimum is the scientific name of Basil and the initial idea was to sequence medicinal plants and patent them. 'By the time we were ready, we realized we could no longer do that, as the law had changed,' says Anu. The pivot then was to get into the software business and Ocimum Biosolutions was launched; it went on to become a leader in laboratory information management systems.

Sometimes, macro-environment or technology changes perforce companies to pivot. History notes countless examples of well-funded companies collapsing because they couldn't morph their business models in the face of changing technology.

Rajesh Jain started Netcore in late-1998, after he sold IndiaWorld. For the first eight to 10 years, Netcore tried many things; they created a blog search engine, got into RSS aggregation, but none of these worked. In Rajesh's words: 'I realized if Netcore had to grow, there was a need for a fundamental pivot and it had to have two sides: one, the product journey and the two, the management journey. These two pivots laid the foundation of Netcore.'

He further adds, 'Once we got the CEO, I stepped back. You cannot have two people driving the business. I had to get out of the way as I was good at ideation but maybe not in execution. On the product side, we launched a few products; one of them was an SMS-based service providing daily free SMS of news, cricket score, Bollywood releases, etc. In 2007–08, the prices of SMS suddenly went up 10 times and we had to discontinue the services overnight. It was the only time in my life when we were burning cash. The price went up from 1 paise to 10 paise overnight. But we realized that all is not lost. To survive, we needed to pivot again and understood what our core strength was. We had the capacity of sending bulk SMS and we morphed the business to the enterprise segment. That worked and we became an enterprise solutions company. Then we added mailer services and for our clients we started to provide email and SMS marketing. In 2014–15, we came across marketing automation and started on that journey to further deepen our engagement with our customers. Today, Netcore is the largest full-service marketing technology company in India.'

Summarizing the constant pivots, Netcore took to stay ahead of the game, 'In the product track you have to keep listening to customers, the problems they are facing. If you observe them and try to listen, you will find opportunity,' shared Rajesh.

One of the things that Rajesh said and which stuck to me as I wrote this book is that as an entrepreneur, you have to keep thinking of what's next on the horizon, you have to keep thinking of something new. Entrepreneurs should be paranoid, because there are smarter people out there and they can beat you at your game.

Founders in the growth phase of start-ups are laser focused on their own company: its product, people and strategy. This is what makes founders obsessive but it also means that start-ups tend to operate in a vacuum and in isolation. One of the pitfalls of this is while the founders are aware of the competition, they tend not to focus attention on competitive analysis and thus, have blind spots, which suddenly spring surprises when the start-ups least expect it.

As they say, keep friends close but enemies closer. Founders need to be aware of what their competition is doing. They need to be totally aware of the competitor's products and services and should regularly be users of their competitors' services to gauge their offerings.

It also helps if your competition is another start-up, to have friendly discourse. More often than not, this can help both the start-ups and it helps consolidate the market in the initial days when you don't want price wars which could kill both the businesses. While it is important not to duplicate the others' products offerings, it doesn't also mean that certain best practices should be copied.

DAVID AND GOLIATH

As entrepreneurs, you also have to be wary of both David and Goliath.

Often, on seeing the success of a start-up in a particular domain, a large Goliath starts entering the market. While the start-up can remain agile and try to stay ahead in the game, the founders needs to be aware that the scale of the market might change and they need to take a strategic decision regarding the direction of their business.

When I was building Recreate Solutions, we operated and dominated a niche which was providing broadcast technology solutions to global broadcast giants like EchoStar, Sky, etc. Also, at the time, typically, large organizations had two offices that looked into the technology landscape of the firm: the chief technology officer (CTO) and the chief information officer (CIO). Our solutions would be a part of the chief technology officers (CTO) mandate of the client organization as we brought deep domain expertise, which the company had built over its seven-year journey.

On the other hand, the CIO's side of the business dealt with the large Indian IT services companies who provided Enterprise Resource Planning (ERP), Customer Relationship Management (CRM) and other pure-play enterprise solutions. In the case of a particular client based in Denver, Recreate was the technology solution provider for the CTO's business, while one of India's largest IT services company provided several multi-million-dollar services in ERP and data warehousing solutions to the same customer. They tried to enter our more profitable business unsuccessfully. They couldn't fathom why a large enterprise would take the services of a six-year-old start-up. They then did what large enterprises do best when they can't win clients directly; they started hiring key technical architects and project managers from my company at much higher salaries.

I soon realized that either I would need to change gear, raise substantial capital to fight this billion-dollar behemoth that was looking to build a media entertainment practice or I would use this as an opportunity and exit. I did the latter and within seven months, found a US systems integrator as an acquirer of the business.

Just as in my case, there was a 'Goliath' circling me, start-ups in a state of growth need to be aware of smaller 'Davids' who will provide the latest solutions and attract the same customers that you are after. Often, larger start-ups scoff at newbie start-ups who soon take market-share from them. And as the adage goes, 'If you cannot beat them, join them,' and in such cases one should look at acquiring these newer start-ups and consolidate your market.

I return to Anu's entrepreneurial journey, where, early on in its growth journey, Ocimum opted for mergers and acquisitions as the mode for growth. They went on to acquire three international firms to become a globally integrated genomics firm. Organically, Ocimum was thriving well, but as Anu mentioned, they wanted to be more than a bioinformatics company, 'We wanted to be the lab-next-door that could provide a researcher with services across the spectrum in a timely and cost-effective manner.'

The goals in front of Ocimum then were—a strong presence in the US, expansion of their portfolio of services to include biomarker discovery, and a customer base in Europe. 'We realized growth through acquiring assets seemed like a great way to build a large, scalable and sustainable company, so long as the pieces fit with our proprietary Research-as-a-Service (RaaS) business model. Ultimately, we achieved these goals through a combination of organic growth and three mergers.'

Anu however cautions start-ups that are too eager to grow fast. 'You'll also need to consider another kind of cost, beyond purchase price, when contemplating a merger: running costs. You'll need to make sure you can contain running costs of adding the new acquisition by finding synergies and increasing revenues. You should focus on sales force synergies (if either company has a product or service), general and administrative savings and operational efficiencies that can be derived from a merger. Cutting these can help you keep all the benefits of the new acquisition but stunt the cost of running a company now made larger,' she elaborates.

Mergers and acquisitions (M&As) do have benefits in terms of the positive change they bring to the organization. 'In our first acquisition, one of the benefits that we greatly underestimated was the buzz created by the MWG acquisition, which led to instant name recognition and customer access worldwide for Ocimum. We received a similar boost when we incorporated Gene Logic into our business; indeed, we retained Gene Logic's name to capitalize on the genomics goodwill associated with the brand,' says Anu.

She also agrees that not all M&As are successful. Even at Ocimum, one acquisition did not pan out as planned due to cultural issues. 'But each acquisition was a learning experience, and by our third M&A, the process was smoother. Amalgamation of disparate entities—be it MWG, Isogen or Gene Logic—is possible only because of complementary competencies and customer bases. Ocimum has graduated from being a small bioinformatics company in India to being a leading, integrated, global, one-stop solution provider for genomics,' added Anu.

Acquisition should be an integral part of the strategy of growth of the companies especially in today's dynamic world, with access to capital for right decisions that would boost growth opportunities for start-ups.

BEING START-UP BATTLE READY

- Entrepreneurs need to be able to adapt to changing business paradigms and not be hardnosed about earlier decisions.
- Don't be afraid to accept 'pivots'.
- Pivots do not imply that earlier decisions were wrong, but reflect the fact that the business is adapting to market conditions and data.
- Share the reasons of pivot openly with the team, along with all data.
- Defining a narrow and focused target market is key for initial success. You cannot be everything to everyone.
- Acquisition strategy is an integral part of enhancing the market penetration and width.

9

IT IS A NO, TILL THE MONEY HITS THE BANK

Now that the business has matured, you should be looking to raise capital to be able to scale up. Raising VC at this stage is different from raising money at the angel stage. At the angel stage, as has been mentioned before, the investors mostly take a bet on the entrepreneur.

The institutional VCs look at businesses with more rigour. Given that you have been running the business for a few years and have the insight of the early metrics, the process this time round would involve a deep dive into the business dynamics and the clear articulation of growth path.

At this stage of the business, we at Unicorn Ventures look at the following determinants:

- Determine that there is a big and growing market.
- Determine the product differentiator and the moat of the business in the face of competition.
- Determine the strength of the management team besides the core founding team.
- Determine how the company fits in with the investment philosophy of the fund.
- Determine the business projections based on the present metrics and solid historical evidence.
- Determine the rationale and the thought behind the use of the capital raised.

- Determine in the longer term, how the investors will get an exit and the overall strategic direction of the business.

I am often asked how companies need to approach the various rounds of funding. Once a business has developed a track record (an established user base, consistent revenue figures or some other key performance indicator), the company is primed for Series A funding in order to further monetize its user base and product offerings. In this round, it's important to have a plan for developing a business model that will be sustainable in the long run.

Seed start-ups have great ideas that generate substantial numbers of enthusiastic users, but the company does not know how it can monetize the business. In Series A funding, investors are not only looking for great ideas, but a strong strategy for turning that idea into a successful, money-making business.

Series B rounds are all about taking businesses to the next level, past the development stage. Investors help start-ups get there by expanding market reach. Companies that have gone through seed and Series A funding rounds have already developed substantial user bases and have proven to investors that they are prepared for success on a larger scale.

Series B funding is used to grow the company so that it can meet these levels of demand. Building a winning product and growing a team requires quality talent acquisition. Bulking up on business development, sales, advertising, tech, support and employees calls for serious investments. Series B is often led by many of the same characters as the earlier round, including a key anchor investor who helps to draw in other investors.

Businesses that make it to Series C funding sessions are already quite successful. These companies look for additional funding to help them develop new products, expand into new markets or even to acquire other companies. In Series C rounds, investors inject capital in a successful business in an effort to receive lesser risk substantial returns. Series C funding is focused on scaling the company, growing as quickly and as successfully as possible.

One possible way to scale a company could be to acquire another company. As the operation gets less risky, newer genres of investors come into play. In Series C, groups such as hedge funds, investment banks, private equity firms and large secondary market groups alongside the traditional VCs look at investments. The reason for this is that the company has already proven itself to have a successful business model; these new investors come to the table expecting to invest significant sums of money into the company to take into a leadership position.

Some companies can go on to Series D, E and further rounds of funding. For the most part, though, companies gaining up to hundreds of millions of dollars in funding through Series C rounds are prepared to continue to develop on a global scale. Companies that do continue with Series D funding are already near unicorns and they then have a different path either to IPO or to be acquired by large players. After having raised so much capital, these companies usually become 'too large to fail' and often even in distress sale situation have some value for some buyer.

BANK ON BANKERS

A topic that generates enough debate whenever broached is whether entrepreneurs should do the fundraise directly or engage with advisors and bankers in the process. My personal view on this varies. If the company is in the early-stages, the entrepreneur must do the fundraise themselves.

In fact, at Unicorn India Ventures, we stay away from deals that are brought to us by bankers or advisors. There is a two-fold reason for this: first, these deals are not proprietary and the real value of an early-stage investor is in being able to source deals that are proprietary in nature. Also, at the early-stage, you need to see the drive in the entrepreneur to be able to reach out, make cold calls and send emails to the investors. This shows that they have the extra drive and fighter's spirit that is required for surviving in the bruising journey of entrepreneurship. During the early-stage rounds, the investors back the founder and the idea rather than the detailed business model and therefore the need is for the founder to be at the left, right and centre of the fundraise.

The second reason why you don't need banker or advisor in the initial stages is because the angel and seed investors are themselves involved with the fundraise and they not only open doors but work with the founder in finetuning the proposition.

However, the scenario starts to change as one goes to the later stages of fundraise. As the company evolves and as it goes through the subsequent process of fundraise, there comes a need for an investment banker. Bankers work closely with the founders and articulate the entrepreneurs' visions in terms that the VCs understand. Often, the growth plans and the vision of the start-up is on the top of the mind of the founder and the bankers act as catalysts in getting that scripted. Moreover, since bankers do this for a living, they have a deep understanding of various models and are good at macro analysis of the industry and draw parallels from the global context.

Whether you end up working with investment bankers or not, there is plenty you can learn from them. Anyone with a positive attitude can begin networking, and what makes investment bankers excel at networking is that they have the patience to cultivate those relationships over time. They realize that who you know is as important as what you know. The reward is that bankers have a good insight into what investors want and expect from start-ups. Bankers have a lot of experience in analyzing the viability of a start-up and whether it will be a success, and through their networks, they know what questions VCs will ask of start-up founders. In essence, good investment bankers know the criteria needed to get VCs onboard. Learning these skills and applying them to your business can help you target specific investors with relevant pitches.

MONEY IN THE BANK OR SIFTING WHEAT FROM CHAFF

Founders need to be conscious of certain hairy points when going through the VC rounds. They need to check directly or through the bankers if their business model fits the investment thesis and stage of the VC. Else, it will be a lot of work in futility.

VCs always like to look at and understand newer business models. Analysts and associates in VC firms are mandated to study newer business models. These young, sharp and dynamic professionals who are knowledge-hungry seek constant answers from the founders. While sometimes, this also helps to sharpen the thought process of the founders, they can often lead to waste of time and so, founders initially must try to determine the 'real' level of interest. This is another area where the expertise of the advisors comes into play.

There will be situations when the founders should go by the old adage, 'If it is too good to be true, then it possibly is too good to be true.' If you get a term-sheet (initial offer) which is better than your expectations and far exceeds what others have offered, do not get excited and carried away but look at it very skeptically. Often, the investor in this case is fishing around to understand more and tie the founder up in an 'exclusive period' but eventually, will not close the deal. Or it could be a case that the investor has not understood the business, and the plan would unravel during the detailed due diligence process that would follow. It could also be that the investor is new in the business and wants to make a deal or two and is therefore, eager to ensure that they can close the deal. In any case, whatever be the reason, a founder needs to tread carefully in such circumstances and not get excited by the outlier offer.

And finally, a transaction isn't complete till the money hits the bank.

There are various hoops a founder needs to go through before they can close a VC funding. These involve initial contact with the VC, initial discussion with VC team on business, initial due diligence with the associates of the VC firm, meeting with the Partners of the Fund, getting a non-binding term sheet, detailed process of due diligence (DD) in terms of financial DD, legal DD and commercial DD, which involves talking to customers, getting into detailed negotiation on various aspects of the transaction, shareholders agreement discussion and negotiation, having pre-closure conditions, signing the agreement between all shareholders which involves the old and new shareholders, and finally disbursal of money from the VCs. This entire process can take anywhere between three to six months and right through the process, there is always chances of slippage.

The founder and the advisor must stay on top of the transaction during the entire process. It becomes even more complex if there are discussions between the existing investors and the new investors. Often deals fall flat not because the investor did not like the plan or the valuation, but over peripheral rights like Board Membership and other rights or certain objections taken by existing investors.

Fundraising does not happen in isolation. It happens alongside the day-to-day business. The founders thus, have to balance the growth of the company as well as manage the fundraising process. Do not forget, while you are doing that, the potential investors are closely monitoring the business progress. During the process, the business metrics must also be in line as had been projected, and if there is strong negative variance then the investors 're-look at the deal'.

Fundraising is an art which all successful entrepreneurs must master. It doesn't come easily to most technology entrepreneurs, but they must learn how to navigate the entire process again and again to be able to raise substantial capital to be able to scale up.

NEUTRAL AND DREAM

The life of the entrepreneur changes after a VC gets on board. Be careful in deciding the VC. Big brand VCs aren't always the best. You need a VC who understands you, the business and who can add value. Therefore, think hard on the journey with a VC and the type of VC you want as an investor.

Says Abhinay Choudhari, 'I think all investors are generally aligned. They are only concerned when the company is not growing according to the planned trajectory. Fortunately for us, our business plans were very realistic. We never had issues with any investor and hence, there was a high degree of alignment. We were also not eyeing higher valuations. Our focus was always on realistic growth and realistic valuations. This helped us in getting a very co-operative board.'

Abhinay acknowledges that while they were raising funds there were enough big and branded players who wanted to invest, but somehow, they never felt the need to reach out to them, and hence they had smaller investors but who understood their business and vision. 'I think that is an important lesson for an entrepreneur. Challenges also arise if you have a very dominating fund house as a board member and they begin to call the shots and try and change the business model. So, thankfully that did not happen. The last round of funds that we raised, we did get a big name on the board, Alibaba. But, thankfully beyond their participations in Board Meetings they have let us run the show,' says Abhinay.

According to Phani, founder of Redbus, 'Most of the investors are good. There are some who are difficult to work with. I would recommend entrepreneurs to do a quick reference check about the investor that they may have finalized to get on board. It really helps. While in our case, we were lucky to have a board and investor that kept the communication doors open, but in some of the companies I have seen investors causing problems and in one case the founders decided to shut operations as they could not get on with an investor.'

Getting the right investor is very important. The founders are young and they need help from investors especially if it's their first company. In your first stint you really don't know many things, how to network or build a product roadmap, plan strategy, etc. Whereas VCs are part of bigger network and they have a wealth of experience. They can take your start-up journey from zero to the next level.

I categorize VCs into three buckets: first are the 'dream VCs'. These are the people who will go out of their way to help you. They make the right directions and are good to deal with when it comes to interpersonal relationships.

Then there are the 'neutral VCs'—having them on board won't hurt you. And then there are the third kind who are negative to have, for instance, a company where the VC keeps dilly-dallying on decisions taken by the founder.

These things come out in reference checks. I think it is a must-do because the VCs will be part of your journey. You need to be sure of VC just as the VC needs to be sure of you and the business.

Post the rounds of funding, the entrepreneur must develop skills in the management of the board and manage the interplay between various investors. Most founders aren't exposed to this side of business and are busy building the product and defining the market in the initial years, but after the later stages of funding they suddenly realize that they are responsible to a professional board of the investors.

What is further intriguing to many is that not all investors have the same agenda. The early-stage investors who have been in the business for long often want to exit the business, while the later investors want to build the business. Often the relationship between earlier investors and the founders get strained as the earlier investors feel neglected in the eyes of the founder, as they have passed their 'sell by date'. Again, certain investors might want to change the management team and get a professional CEO to replace the founder. These have been dealt with later in the book, but the founders need to be cognizant of these facts when they embark on the fundraising path.

So, think ahead and think hard before you embark on the path of institutional fundraise.

BEING START-UP BATTLE READY

- Be prepared before you meet investors, as you have just one shot to make an impression.
- In the later rounds of funding, you need to have professional advisors.
- Speak to other founders and be aware of the hairy points that having a VC entails for you and the business.
- Go for a VC who understands you and the business, rather than a branded VC.
- If something sounds too good, then it most likely is not real.
- Nothing is closed till the money hits the bank.

10

BEWARE OF THE FUNDING FRANKENSTEIN, IT CAN KILL YOU AND THE BUSINESS

Founders need to have a sense of equanimity and focus on building the business as the raison d'etre of their existence. Sometimes, founders handle the lows when their chips are down well, but flounder when the going gets good. This may sound surprising but is often true. When a founder is starting up, the start-up is the pivot around which their entire life revolves. The launch of the product, the building of their team and talking to investors subsumes them day in and day out.

The closing of a substantial fundraise round is so epochal in the life of the founder that it almost leads to a new state of mind. Post fundraise, the upheaval that a founder faces within an organization and in personal life is momentous. The founder needs to be able to adjust to the changed circumstances for the company to emerge from the growth stage to the consolidation phase.

Given the challenges of fundraising and the euphoria post the success, it is simply human nature for founders to get carried away. I know of a few instances when a founder, after raising large tranche of money, has gone astray and lost the moral and emotional compass that made them who they were. In the initial days, the founders would boot-strap. They would work at less than market salaries and would invariably travel by cheapest means available. They would dress modestly and stay away from brands. They would make intense sacrifices for the company they had founded and were building. They survive for months on end without salaries to help the company tide over the cash-flow pressures. In fact, they would use their personal credit card for company expenses and not get reimbursed. This is the life-story of every start-up founder.

Often, large fund-raising rounds are followed by extensive media coverage and hype. Start-up founders find their pictures plastered on the front pages of magazines and newspapers and overnight they are elevated to the position of a 'demi-god' by the media. Even the sanest founder starts to suffer from the 'I am the new God in town' syndrome.

This pushes some founders to make rapid changes in their lifestyles, like their style of dressing and their behavior, and they start getting spotted in celebrity parties. They want to maintain a high profile constantly and aspire to become the media's poster boys. In the new-found limelight, they change their core character. Within the industry, it is common knowledge that there are a number of cases where sensible and rational founders, from the humblest backgrounds, lost their moorings and this created strife in their personal and professional lives. Their spouses and family members could not keep up with the rapidly changing reality and this often lead to divorces or bitter personal lives. All this causes the entrepreneur to lose the sharp business focus that had brought them success so far. This is the first sign of trouble and soon the cookie starts to crumble.

This is where the investors, mentors, co-founders and advisors have a role to play and need to speak directly with the founder and convey that the funding rounds are only the beginning of the race. While the newer equity infusion in the company will give them slightly better salaries and lessen their personal pain to some extent, they must be driven by the equity they hold. Investors must ensure that the compensation a founder draws in terms of salary remains lower than what it would have been had they been in a job. Till exit, founders always need to be driven by the equity.

Phanindra Sama, the humble and brilliant founder of Redbus says, 'Of course, yes. If the equity ownership goes down too low, it kills the founder's motivation. Hence one needs to be very careful while diluting. However, I must say that I was offered some equity back (based on milestones) during our Series B fundraise. The same was also on the cards when we were raising the next round. I think investors do understand that if the equity ownership goes too low, it can demotivate founders. Hence, they try to give it back in later rounds. But it is best to be mindful of dilution from early on.'

Another common mistake founders make post funding rounds, that is not only detrimental to the growth of the business but sometimes even kills the company, is to believe that convincing investors and raising funding somehow ensures their projections will become the reality. If the company had raised funding based on a plan that says the business will be worth ₹500 crore from the present ₹100 crore within three years post funding; many first-time founders immediately begin to acquire what a ₹500 crore business would need—a larger office, a head of corporate development, a CFO who has managed ₹500 crore business—as if the funding has ensured the end goal. Inexperienced founders confuse the act of raising capital with achievement of the business plan. My advice to entrepreneurs would be to not let the success of fundraise effect your self-esteem to such an extent that your ego takes precedence and the steps that you have taken to move from zero to five or six go in vain.

I sometimes blame the VCs in such situations as well. Driven by their desire for growth and subsequent rounds of funding at enhanced valuations, they push the founder towards taking some of these decisions. While the board will encourage growth, you as the founder and CEO will need to have the necessary financial wisdom and responsibility to understand that this is an ongoing process and never the end. The matured and seasoned founder will have the gumption to tell the VC and the board to back off slightly and define their own pace. This remains the biggest challenge post funding—the art of taking your start-up to a scaleup.

I have made this mistake as an entrepreneur. When you have many ideas to scale up and strive long for a funding round and when it happens, you start firing from many cylinders—from too many cylinders, actually. What one needs to realize is that the organization is a living and breathing entity and it cannot undertake a sudden step change. I have made the mistake of hiring too many new personnel at senior positions without giving them time to embed, the mistake of starting too many service lines and regional offices simultaneously.

These often break the backbone of the business. And one observes that this additional funding, instead of bringing growth, creates internal strife, confusion in the business direction the company is taking and personnel unrest. Often, the original team that was there with the founder leaves post funding as they cannot adjust to the change. These were the trusted folks who had helped bring the company to the present level, believing in the founder. The newer hires, with their more structured approach, slowly realize that in the start-up, their efforts won't help to change the needle as the start-up is still very early in terms of process and product and their efforts won't to be able to make substantial changes. Eventually, they leave in frustration.

In short, post the funding round that the founder strived for and worked hard to close, the situation of the company is far worse. On top of it, they face constant pressure from the investors. Suddenly, within months of raising funding, they wish they had not raised the funding and want to turn the clock to the pre-funding days.

THE COMPANY DOESN'T BELONG TO THE 'FOUNDER'

Founders should realize that post the rounds of funding, the company doesn't belong to the 'founder'. The company now has a professional board, representing the investors who have a say in the running of the business. This needs a lot of adjustment in the mind of the founder, who still tends to treat it like their own fiefdom. This is among the first challenges the founders face from the start-up phase to the growing up phase. Founders who cannot adjust to this 'new normal' will exit from the management positions during the Consolidation Phase.

It is also a fact that once the VCs gain a foothold in the company and the product/service has matured to a stable stage, chances are that an 'outsider' can be roped in to be the CEO of the company and the founder can either get a seat on the board depending on the stake of equity he has, or he has to be asked to go. Apple is an apt example of this. Steve Jobs and Steve Wozniak, the founders of Apple, were not on the board when the company went public. They were both just employees with good designations and their joint stake in the company was down to a mere 23 per cent.

To have a professional board at an early stage is actually good for the business and the team of founders. For young entrepreneurs with no prior experience of running a business, the board can be a good sounding board as well as a place where they can get the knowledge of the nitty-gritties of setting up a business.

However, there are a few basic rules for a founder to understand about the investor board is:

Don't Surprise the Board Even If It Is Good News: No board likes surprises. Always keep them informed of any impending bad news. The earlier the news is broken, the better it is. The board is rational and has folks who understand that sometimes, despite best efforts, plans don't get executed. But hoping for things to change and not informing the board will only lead to distrust. Even pleasant surprises are frowned upon. So, if there is a new change of direction or addition of a service-line, keep the board informed as they don't want to be taken for granted.

Don't Ask the Board to Solve Your Problems: I have seen this in some of the first-time founders amongst my investee companies, who feel that the board is the panacea for all problems the company faces. They look to the board for solutions. What I hate to hear in board meetings from founders is, 'What do we do next?' The board expects founders to have an array of potential solutions and to be able to discuss the same with the board. The board needs to view the founder as decisive and in control of the business. Not always seeking direction from the board. Having said that, the board is always there to help you directionally.

Understand Each Board Member's Perspective: The board at the end of the day is made of disparate folks, who have different skillsets and priorities. In order to get the maximum out of them, the founder needs to understand the board members better.

CURE FOR ALL ILLS

I have seen many a founder struggle with the board dynamics post the funding. This could be because either the founder does not appreciate the fiduciary responsibility and the authority of the board or believes that it is there to be the cure for all ills. Disagreements with the board members are inevitable, the founders' responsibility is to resolve them amicably.

Phani of Redbus believes that balancing these relationships is extremely important. 'In my case, I enjoyed a very good rapport with my investors. They allowed me the freedom to make a decision by myself. I would listen to all of them (and their variety of perspectives) and make a decision that best suits the company. The investors didn't mind if I wasn't doing what they wanted. There was mutual respect. I think entrepreneurs can benefit a lot by cultivating such rapport with the investors,' he adds.

Abhishek Negi, founder of Eggoz, explains that in the initial days, the investors are involved in everything, meetings and calls happen every day or week. As things move up and the business also stabilizes, the meeting may happen once a month or once a quarter, but the founder should be clear of what he wants. 'I think as entrepreneurs, one should be clear about what they want from their investors. My co-founders and I have been clear that investors will not call the shots. Investors should give their comments/advice and provide a satellite view of the market or the issue being discussed, but business will not run according to them. I have been upfront about it,' shares Abhishek.

The example of Rahul Yadav and Housing.com comes to mind in this regard. From a brilliant young IIT drop-out who created a business in the housing market, he became the symbol of all that could go wrong with a start-up founder and his relation with the board. Rahul who came from a humble background and changed his lifestyle by splurging on a penthouse in the upscale complex of Hiranandani Gardens in Mumbai. This was further augmented when he and co-founders decided to spend a whooping ₹120 crore on a marketing campaign.

He spent over ₹100 crore on a marketing campaign without commensurable results. Clearly, his was a case of believing in the projections without realizing that he had neither the product nor the team to be able to handle this sudden marketing blitzkrieg. He wanted to fast forward the growth and acquire a few smaller competitors but wasn't willing to wait the time and wanted to pay much more than the price.

But the nail in the coffin came when he picked up an open and public spat with the board and to 'mock' them, gave up his holding to the team.

From the poster boy of young entrepreneurship to enfant terrible, the sobriquets that defined Rahul Yadav in 2015 changed dramatically over a few months. It is also a lesson in managing relations between founders and investors/board.

Early that year, a mail he had shot off to investor Shailendra Singh of VC firm Sequoia Capital—threatening to 'vacate the firm' if they didn't stop 'messing around' with him—went public. 'This marks the beginning of the end of Sequoia Cap in India,' wrote Yadav, who was the co-founder of Housing.com at the time. It triggered a downward spiral for the 25-year-old, who first resigned, calling his board members and investors 'intellectually incapable' of having a discussion, then withdrew it before eventually being booted out.

In an interview to *Forbes India* in 2019[10] after nearly four years, Rahul accepted that he was much too young at that time and it was immature behaviour. 'I was a leader in college [IIT Bombay], and then the co-founder of Housing.com. I was always the single point of authority. Even if I was wrong, no one was questioning me. That way, leaders tend to get delusional a bit and take wrong calls with confidence,' he says in the interview.

He also feels that in future if he does again start up he won't get into a spat with investors. 'If there are problems, you have to talk them out. And if things don't work even then, you part ways amicably. Now, I'll do a very good transition,' he said.[11]

It was great to read this interview. Obviously, post the funding rounds of over $130 million, circumstances had taken the better of a young and brilliant person who was exposed to such highs in term of responsibility, capital and media glare. I am sure with these lessons, someone like him will bounce back as a far better entrepreneur in the near future.

Rahul Yadav is perhaps not the lone case of communication breakdown between the founder and the investor. But most founders that I managed

---

[10]'I Was Young and It Was Immature Behaviour: Rahul Yadav.' *Forbes India*. www.forbesindia.com/article/30-under-30-2019/i-was-young-and-it-was-immature-behaviour-rahul-yadav/52507/1. Accessed 21 November 2020.
[11]Ibid.

to speak to for this book and in my personal experience, manage to iron out differences amicably.

BEING START-UP BATTLE READY

- Don't get carried away with the attention you draw post funding and change your core.
- Ramp up the business as you grow to achieve the numbers. Don't assume the numbers will be achieved.
- Post infusion of VC capital, remember you are not the owner of the business but it is the board that represents the company.
- Understanding the board dynamics is an essential part of the role of founder.
- Try to iron out differences with investors, as they also have best interest of company at heart.

11

AS THE COMPANY GROWS, YOU TOO MUST KEEP PACE

Every founder wants to be a Mark Zuckerberg, Elon Musk or Bill Gates, who founded their companies and continued to be the CEOs for a long time. It is interesting to study how the founder's role changes as the business grows.

Anand Deshpande, founder, chairman and MD of Persistent Systems, shared with me the fascinating story of his growth with the company. Persistent was founded in 1990 and, in the initial years, was handling projects in the database segment. One of the reasons for the choice of sector was because Anand had done his PhD on nested relational database and as a part of that, worked on indexing, query processing and complex objects, and he did not want to compromise his resume. But after six to seven years, in an internal meeting, some of the employees asked him, 'This is what you are doing for yourself. What is in it for us?'

'People had questions about the long-term vision of the company, finances, etc.' shared Anand. And this question got him thinking on a 'my company or our company' shift.

'In the first seven to eight years of Persistent, I was not looking at building a company. I started Persistent with some interesting work from people I knew. We were in a niche area, doing some really high-end work. I was involved in coding for each project and I liked the work we were doing, but then other people didn't necessarily want to work in that area,' says Anand.

It took time for Anand to realize that the company and he were two individual entities. 'The conversation with team mates made me think on the transition from "my company to our company". It took six months to a year to get used to the concept that the company and I are two entities. I also realized that I cannot let my agenda drive the company, it should be the other way. This transition also meant I should get into broader areas of work, so yes, I like coding but there are smarter people who can do it and we hired them. This also meant I had to focus on growing the sales process,' says Anand.

He also told me that he was always more the CEO of the company than a founder, the difference was that before this transition, it was his vision for himself that was driving the company. 'Once I decided to transition my target, the CEO's job also changed. It was not restricted to just me now, but to a much broader company whose vision was much broader than my vision,' he shares.

One piece of advice that Anand shares with me as companies scale is that every company goes through an 'S' curve. As a company you start something, grow the business, then the growth flattens and you need to find the next S curve to grow again. Persistent Systems is in its fourth 'S' curve.

'Companies do not run in a linear way. The way you run the business changes and it's very hard for founders to transition from one to another. In every S curve we have had a different business model, different growth pattern, and there is a little bit of discontinuity as the model changes, etc. It's pretty difficult to move from one orbit to the second and then the third. At every orbit, you need to do different sets of things, you need to bring in new energy into the system. And every time you do this, you run a risk of failing. So, the risk is higher at that time when you are going through the transition,' says Anand.

Persistent's growth and the role of Anand is about realizing what is good for the company, adapting to that change as a founder-cum-CEO and learning from it.

The only way that a founder can continue to run his business is by adapting and learning. The changing role of the founder of a business is something that I have lived through myself, during my days as the founder of Recreate Solutions.

It is the passion, the excitement, the swagger, and the self-belief that are essential to get a business off the ground. However, the same emotions can come back to haunt a founder in the later phases. I speak from personal experience on that front too.

VC investors feel that often founders are not ideally suited to take on leadership roles within a business if that business is to scale. It's believed that only 50 per cent of founders continue to be the CEOs of their firm seven-eight years after multiple rounds of funding has been raised, and for those who try to scale their business and get to an IPO, only 25 per cent make it to that level.

When you start from nothing, you are anonymous, very few people know about your business. Over time, you build that into a successful corporation/listed entity, but then come along other vagaries. Though you created the organization from nothing, you need to slowly give away your control to other stakeholders, like investors, shareholder, employees, etc. Though you may be successful, as an individual, you will be back at nothing.

FOUNDER TO LEADER

Most founders will often find themselves beyond their skillsets when they need to put structures and hierarchies and processes in place that will enable the business to progress to the next level. Success makes the founder less and less qualified to carry out the duties required of them.

One other thing to recognize is that the business will often take on some or many proclivities of the founder—both their skills and weaknesses. This creates a kind of debt within the business. A founder will try to learn on the go, will want to have a finger in every pie but in reality, a founder doesn't need to do and know everything. It is still a hard lesson for a founder to understand.

These are some of the reasons why when investors are involved in a business, at some point or another, the founder who has grown with the company will be told, 'Thank you for making the business a success but we're going to have to let you go from your present role.'

It's never easy. Whether it's something the founder comes to terms with or whether they are told they have to go, it's going to be problematic. It could take months for the transition, and they could be a thorn in the side of the board for months and years, even if they are given a new position within the company. Always remember your emotional health is going to affect the business and the people within it. Learn to become more self-aware and more company aware. And celebrate when the business you founded grows beyond you.

Based on my experiences as a founder and some of the traits that make this role transition easier based on the interactions I have had with some successful founders of large enterprises, are:

- Learning to Delegate
  Learning to delegate responsibilities becomes a major part of your job as a founder. For founders who like doing everything themselves and think they can handle it all, this can be a difficult step. But hiring the best talent you can find and people who really believe in your mission and what you are trying to accomplish will make it easier to let go of some things so you can start focusing on growing the business. Remember, delegating isn't just about telling others what to do, but also about *empowering* your team and showing trust in them. Allowing others to make decisions, and facilitating those decisions along the way will help your team become more comfortable doing so.
  Anu Acharya explains how she works and when she decides to delegate, 'I get very involved during the early stages. When we first start doing something, I need to know it inside out, but once its stable and its smoothly running, I move back and that particular vertical or segment head takes over. That's my way of working,' she said.
- Manage the Flow of Information
  As you begin hiring more and more people, you will also realize that every detail about the company is no longer in your brain. Figuring out the best way to manage the knowledge flow in your company and making sure your team knows how to efficiently

access and communicate this information will help make the
transition easier.

In one of my conversations with Abhinay Choudhari, co-founder
BigBasket, which saw rapid growth once it raised funds, he said
that creating a culture of your own helps when you are rapidly
growing. 'We documented all our company culture and made sure
that everyone understood it, would accept it and work accordingly,'
said he. This helped the company to move faster as well.

- Face Yourself

You need to be unbelievably ruthless about what's working and
what's not working. As CEO, you will have to change hundreds of
times to face the different challenges in the different stages your
business will go through. There should be no fear or shame in
accepting failures and pivoting the business.

Rajat Mohanty of Paladion said that even if you have disagreements
with co-founders, you need to stand your ground. 'There are two
situations which need to be tackled head-on: one, when there is a
disagreement over the direction of the business; and two, the co-
founder's inability to scale up. In our case the first case happened,
we had a difference of opinion on the direction of business. The
difference of opinion happened due to the disagreement on
product roadmap and the direction to be taken,' he shared.

One of the things that can help is having an advisor around who
may help ease this process.

- Learn Not Just the P&L but Also the Balance Sheet

All founders have an inherent understanding of the profit and
loss (P&L) statement, whether they come from the technical or
the product side of the business, or the sales and marketing side.
What they often lack is an understanding of the balance sheet
side of the business—how the funding cycle changes the balance
sheet dynamics, what the off-balance sheet items are, how does
capitalization of assets and IPS impact the valuation. This is the
area where not only a CFO needs to help out, but the founder
needs to understand these in details. Phanindra Sama founder of
Redbus, while sharing his journey as an entrepreneur for this book,

told me that he had no background of finance, so the moment they hired a CFO, he spent a considerable amount of time learning the nuances of the financial world.

In an interesting chat with Aniruddha Sharma, co-founder of Carbon Clean Solutions, on the changing roles as the start-up started to scale, he said, 'I found myself quickly changing from an active, hands-on role in the building of our product to a leadership role where I needed to direct and motivate our growing team as we scaled our business. There is a common belief that founders aren't the best at taking on the leadership role needed to scale and that many start-ups that scale the right way will eventually surpass the capabilities of their founders. The main reason is that successful founders must learn to adapt, or they can be quickly left behind. Some of the most successful start-ups have reached maximum potential because their founders took on the CEO role completely, and they knew they needed to evolve and grow with the needs of their business,' he said.

MANY HATS

As I write this part of the chapter, I reminisce over my journey as a start-up founder, raising the first money and growing the business to employ over 400 people.

As the founder, I used to wear a lot of hats. I would do bits of everything and no job was too small or too big. I was based in London and the operations were headquartered in India. When I would visit the operations in Mumbai, I would joke around, pull someone's leg and everyone would laugh. We were a small group of around 20 people, all working to build a service for the media industry. Each of us knew everything that was going on and there was little to no politics.

As the company grew and we added around 30 people, I began to split departments and this was our first split in reporting lines. Depending on the industry, it may be engineers and operations, or hardware and software, everyone is busy, everyone knows everybody and there is little need for company security, assets are easy to manage and track, benefits and payroll are not that hard, and at this stage I began to think I needed someone in HR and payroll. Till then, someone on the financial side of the company was handling those responsibilities. Things that did not pertain to technology or sales was handled by the finance person.

When the team grew to around 60 people, things took a drastic turn. This is around the stage when it became impossible for everyone to know everything that was happening in the company in real time. I didn't know the other employees as well and started to think more about our culture because the two new departments were hiring completely different sets of people for the first time. The company now needed a full-time HR and a full-time accounting department. This meant I needed real leaders, and I found out that some of the initial hires and pillars of the organization could be good at certain things but couldn't manage a team of more than three, when the demand was that they manage 10–15. I started to feel the need for a COO to manage the operations, as I would be focused on external matters more.

This is the stage, where I, the CEO, suddenly found myself pulled in multiple directions at all hours and had to begin to shed responsibilities to a newly hired COO, and felt the need for an admin to control traffic and maximize time. When any company grows to around 100 plus, the demands change in the life of the CEO. I had to be particularly good at articulating the company message, managing larger, more sophisticated clients and speaking the language of a senior team who is also growing in sophistication.

Everyone—your investors, employees and clients—all expect a lot more of you, so you must rise to the occasion. One is constantly in meetings, pouring over financials, thinking about strategy and dealing with competitors.

You are having to rehearse more speeches, deal with media and learn to talk in clear concise soundbites. Suddenly, everything you wear, say and do at every hour of the day and night matters. You begin to recognize that you're responsible for a lot of assets, shareholders, company property, people, their livelihoods and all that goes with it. You lay awake at night more often, worried about the responsibility, yet they are exciting times too. By then, somewhere along that path, you realize that the role is bigger than you. Even the little things you never had to worry about earlier can make or break someone else's day, so you must be sure to greet everyone and always look as steady as possible.

Even something as simple as an office move becomes overly complicated because of space and location requirement and the timing between one lease and another, not to mention the plans for future growth. How much space do you take? All of this becomes an endless series of meetings, not to mention the constant adjustments to the organization chart while still circling through all ranks to make sure the departments are all working.

I became keenly aware of time. It becomes your most valuable resource and you never have enough of it. I found myself trying to decide if I should hang out with colleagues who now didn't report to me directly. These old hands who did not report to me were still important for their ideas and intel about the course of the business. But I did not want to be seen as partisan and upset the reporting lines. In short, it was a constant period of evolution from the time I was a founder of the business and started hiring folks. Growing a business from one to 500 plus as I did made me constantly evolve myself as the leader of the pack.

I was lucky to have had earlier experience running large franchises as CEO, with over 100 people reporting to me directly or indirectly in the business. Both of them had the same difficulty overall, but fewer skills were needed to run franchises of larger companies, and the sense of responsibility and expectations was greater as the founder of the business.

NIMBLE AND DYNAMIC

The other challenge founders face when the company achieves scale is keeping the start-up and entrepreneurial spirit alive. The systems and processes are in place, the company now has an organization reporting structure, but the founder does not want the company to slow down its responses. The reasons why start-ups scale fast and are constantly able to pivot is because of the nimble and dynamic structure they have. They don't have a cloak of complacency and are seeking out newer opportunities. Founders are under the constant fear that they will lose this 'animal spirit' as the company grows.

The entrepreneurial spirit, as mentioned in earlier chapters, is a mindset. It's an attitude and approach to thinking that actively seeks out change, rather than reacting to change. It is about having an organizational mindset that embraces critical questioning, innovation, service and continuous improvement. It is about taking ownership and pride in your organization.

Anand believes that having a start-up spirit is necessary for every organization irrespective of the size. 'I think companies irrespective of size need to be nimble and agile. When you have a larger company there will be parts of businesses that will be moving faster than the company. Rather, I feel that, sometimes, being a smaller company restricts your pace of growth or scale. For instance, if you see something new in the market and you decide to chase it, if you are a large company you will have the resources to create a front team in no time which will look into it. They have resources to reach customers. A small company will not have this flexibility of mobilizing the resources that quickly. People are already allocated to certain projects. At Persistent too, it is now easier to access resources if we want to start something new, compared to when we were small. That said, getting everybody to move is hard,' shared Anand.

As the start-up up scales up, the entrepreneur needs to nurture the entrepreneurial spirit within their organization and encourage their employees to not only see problems but seek solutions and opportunities. 'Entrepreneurial spirit helps companies grow and evolve rather than become stagnant and stale,' says Phaneesh Murthy, who after his stint in Infosys as head of sales, had been a successful entrepreneur.

It takes work to maintain an entrepreneurial spirit—but all companies can absolutely have it. This gets more challenging as businesses grow—because as they do, there's a tendency to move towards complacency, increased bureaucracy, hierarchy and complexity. Companies start to lose the 'underdog mentality' they started out with, which fueled a fighting, entrepreneurial spirit. And as they grow bigger, businesses may feel they have more to lose than when they started out. This causes them to become more risk-adverse and protective of what they've established. But it's imperative that employers and employees keep their entrepreneurial spirit alive as the organization grows. A company that lost its competitive edge when it was a market leader was Nokia. Once the world-dominant handset maker, it was reduced to rubble as it could not hold against the competition unleashed by Apple and Google.

Some of the steps an entrepreneur must take to foster the entrepreneurial spirit in a company are:

- Inculcate all employees to think like an owner.
- Encourage and champion all ideas.
- Make the culture an integral part of recruitment and only recruit those who have an entrepreneurial spirit.
- Minimize the rules.
- Encourage newer ideas and think out-of-the-box.
- Give people the opportunity to drive change.
- Create a recognition program that rewards people for thinking like an entrepreneur.
- Try to work with colleagues in different departments.
- Always communicate.
- Ask for flexible work options.
- Create a culture of questioning.

HAVE A REWARD SCHEME THAT ENCOURAGES OWNERSHIP AND RECOGNIZES COMPANYWIDE PERFORMANCE

Above all, the founder, even if he becomes CEO of a scaled-up business, must keep his passion alive. His team and organization must remember him as the person who set up the company and built it. While he must induct the core values of a professional CEO, he cannot do away with the attributes that made him the entrepreneur that he is.

An individual who has managed to keep his entrepreneurial spirit alive even after being in the business for more than 50 years is Richard Branson, the serial entrepreneur and founder of the Virgin Group. A quote from his autobiography that inspires me and that founders should hold on to is: 'I view life as one big adventure; I'm always learning, and finding new things to try and challenges to overcome.'[12]

---

[12]Richard Branson. *Finding My Virginity*. Random House UK, 2018.

BEING START-UP BATTLE READY

- Founders of start-ups have to be on a steep learning curve as the company scales up, picking up newer skill sets and organizational building capabilities.
- They must pick up the art of delegation, which is difficult for an entrepreneur who is used to knowing every detail of the company.
- Managing time is key, as you will now have several varied constituents, both within the company and outside, to cater to.
- While you put systems and processes in place, ensure the 'start-up' spirit and drive isn't lost, else you will lose the edge and the driver for retaining key staff.
- As long as you are within the company, keep your personal stamp in the business because the entrepreneur's charisma is best for motivating staff.
- Communicate, communicate and communicate within the company.

12

YOU ARE AS GOOD AS YOU HIRE, SO HIRE RIGHT

If I am asked to pick one task that defines the success of a founder, I would say it is hiring the right people. Whenever I think of team building, I remember how David Ogilvy in *Ogilvy on Advertising* emphasized that recruiting smart people was the key to his company's success.

In the book he says, 'When someone is made the head of an office in the Ogilvy & Mather chain, I send him a Matryoshka doll from Gorky. If he has the curiosity to open it and keep opening it until he comes to the inside of the smallest doll, he finds this message: "If each of us hires people who are smaller than we are, we shall become a company of dwarfs. But if each of us hires people who are bigger than we are, we shall become a company of giants."[13] Russian dolls or Matryoshka dolls are sets of wooden dolls of decreasing size placed inside one another.

Even in the biggest, most stable corporations, putting together a small team can be a perilous process fraught with personality clashes, hierarchical imbalances and conflicting visions. But in a start-up, the challenge of assembling a solid team—and then keeping its members inspired and focused—carries the added stress of being potentially fatal. When a company consists of a half-dozen people, a single recruiting misstep can topple the house.

One of the key differences between creating a team for a start-up versus

---

[13]David Ogilvy. *Ogilvy on Advertising*. Prion, 2011.

creating a team for an ongoing business is the intensity of interaction. If you are on a project team at a major established company, like Infosys, you are not really married to the people on your team. But if you are starting a business and making the first hires, you are looking at one of the most intense relationships you are going to have in your life. It is like marriage. At an Infosys-like organization, there would be more room for error, because the team is more likely to be a small cog in a huge machine.

But with a start-up, it is a life-or-death situation. Issues around power and fairness are prominent, because your entire life is probably vested in the business. You might be living hand-to-mouth while waiting to get funded. With so much at stake, little obstacles are harder to navigate. One of the things that can really break an early-stage team is bringing in the wrong person and then not having any idea how to fire them. That can be a train wreck, especially if there's equity involved.

THE BEST HIRES IN A HYPER-COMPETITIVE WORLD

Today, Infosys is a company of $12.87 billion revenues, with an employee base of 2,42,000 worldwide[14]. However, it has also been through its start-up phase. Early on, the founders of Infosys had realized that they needed to bring in a diverse set of team members to scale up the business and take it to a new direction.

One such person who had been a key hire in the initial days of Infosys was Phaneesh Murthy. In my discussions with Phaneesh for *Everything Started as Nothing* are epitomes of what an early-stage entrepreneurial company needs to do in terms of hiring senior people who come with a different skill-set and background from those that founded the business, and how to ensure a perfect blending of the old and new. His stint also highlights the role of founders and how they should work with new hires.

Since Phaneesh was creating the first sales team for Infosys, he managed to hire many people from his alma mater, IIM Ahmedabad. In the process, he was also creating a sales strategy that was divergently opposite to TCS and Wipro's. 'My approach was we are not selling software;

[14]"History." *Infosys*. www.infosys.com/about/history.html. Accessed 21 November 2020.

we are trying to sell relationships and partnership with other companies. Technically we were trying to marry companies. So, I wanted people who could talk in a senior executive language rather than technical language. I built a different sales and marketing than anyone had in those days. We hired MBAs from all possible industries like consumer product, pharma, financial services, etc. While hiring, I looked for people who had the gumption to win,' says Phaneesh.

When I asked him how he managed to attract talent to an industry which was still nascent, Phaneesh said: 'It was a little bit of a challenge. Other than the fact that I was also from IIM Ahmedabad, I could articulate my vision that Infosys was the new untold land and I sold them the vision of the future and how we will change not the company, but the industry and the nation. Moreover, I put their fears to rest by telling them they were not being hired for their tech skills. We hired them because they were tigers, it's just that the jungle was new.'

Phaneesh's insights tell what an entrepreneurial business needs to do to build a team and scale up. The founders need to have the belief that they need newer hires to scale the business, then they need to make the best hires, not picking those who complement them or are a reflection of their selves. And finally, upon hiring the person, they need to let go and give the person the independence he/she wants, to be able to perform. While building the company is crucial, as Phaneesh rightly mentioned, 'brand building' for a start-up and having the right corporate message are key for getting the best hires in a hyper-competitive world.

He also had some advice for people who are looking to work at start-ups. If you are joining hands with a group of founders, make sure they are people to whom you can look up to and in the process get to learn from them. 'I do not hesitate to admit that I learnt a lot from Mr Murthy and Nandan,' he said.

DISSENTING IDEAS, FLAT STRUCTURES AND QUESTIONING

We are human, and as humans we are wired to be tribal. Tribes are made up of people who share similarities. We naturally like to hire in our own likeness or that of the company's DNA. We feel safe when we flock with people who are similar to us. We find comfort in the feeling that we belong to a team, tribe or community. When we hire from the same business schools, recruit from the same ethnicity and train everyone in the same way, we create a tribe.

Creating a tribe with a common goal and culture is great business practice. However, creating a tribe where everyone thinks the same and avoids dissent, in HR terms is referred to as 'the similarity-attraction effect'. It refers to our tendency to be attracted to people who are similar to us in attitudes, values, preferences and worldview. When we are similar to others, they are more likely to confirm and reinforce our opinions and worldview than to contradict those views. This would suggest they will not prove problematic when we are busy making decisions.

Groupthink occurs in organizations (big and small, but mostly big and non-commercial), when groups prioritize avoiding conflict and reaching consensus over making the best decisions possible. Such decisions are rarely in the interest of the company, rather in the interest of the people within the group. Group members minimize conflict and reach consensus decisions without critically evaluating alternative viewpoints by actively suppressing dissenting viewpoints, and by isolating themselves from outside influences. They do not rock the boat.

They ensure that no-one shouts that the emperor is not wearing any clothes—everyone toes the line and keeps their jobs. There is rarely any ambition in such organizations and rarely any drive, and the talented people leave very quickly. Those that stay become part of the problem. The buck should stop with management, not with the hiring manager. Mediocrity creeps in as managers who fear change and competency hire weaker people.

It was quite interesting to hear Aniruddha Sharma, of Carbon Clean Solutions, talk passionately about his team members, especially when both the founders were close to winding up their start-up. 'Our investors and advisors played a big role in making us understand. Also, some of the early team members that we had also supported us a lot. I can say with immense pride that all my engineers are more qualified than me. Almost 90 per cent are more qualified than me and our CTO, Prateek Bumb (co-founder) and 50 per cent have a PhD focused on what we do,' said he.

A start-up is all about dissenting ideas, flat structures and questioning. It needs diverse philosophies and folks from different backgrounds. Also, a start-up founder needs to be able to handle those coming from different intellectual positions. Entrepreneurs who imbibe this philosophy are able to build better, long-term sustainable organizations. Unlike some industries like banking and consulting where the teams are homogenous, a start-up is a living breathing microcosm that needs creatures of different hues and backgrounds for the microcosm to grow.

These aspects of hiring have to be laid out by the founder. Hiring and building teams in a start-up is the key role of a founder, not of some HR manager and recruiter in the initial days and even later, it is the founder who needs to drive the messaging and the attributes that would lead to making the hires.

Offering an effective compensation plan could be the difference between hiring mediocre employees versus hiring highly effective, driven individuals who can add real value to your start-up. Because the crux of every start-up success story is a strong binding force between the firm's founders and its employees, Employee Stock Options (ESOP) can be the strategic mechanism to build that cohesion, creating shared wealth in the process.

They foster accountability on both sides—employees accelerate past their potential in order to build the best company possible, while founders ensure equitable compensation within the organization. Simply put, everyone wants to be wealthy; ESOPs are just the device to fulfill that desire. ESOPs should be the driver of recruitment; this also shows the mindset of the person you are recruiting.

Some tips for entrepreneurs to structure ESOPs:

- Develop an equity pool at the very beginning of your start-up journey; create a double-digit equity pool rather than a single-digit one.
- Be flexible with your ESOP pattern as you grow—your ESOP offerings should look different at the foundation, growth stages and consolidation stage.
- ESOPs should create value for your employees in the form of

wealth generation; use them as a rewards tool.

- Tweak your ESOPs model as your ability to offer higher salaries expands and your equity capacity narrows.
- Base the offered vesting period on what component of the ESOPs compensation plan is extended to your employee.

HIRE AS IF IT MATTERS

For a founder CEO, hiring is a challenge, but even after hiring, retaining talent is a bigger challenge. For that, it is essential to develop a team culture within a start-up. As a start-up grows under a visionary and aggressive leader, words like 'power' or 'success' to describe a company can sometimes make it easy to imagine a cutthroat environment.

However, a competitive workplace shouldn't run on employees' fear or feel like a real-life Hunger Games. A powerful and successful company operates best and with the most longevity when employees work with a team mentality, each filling a needed role and fulfilling long-term goals.

Here are six things a founder can do to make sure your team is as strong as it can possibly be for your company. This culture should be imbibed deep within the organization, so all line managers also do the same within the hires that they have.

1. Focus on roles: Hiring just to have bodies in the room can harm your team. Companies that do this wind up becoming a revolving door, whether it's because prospective employees see the role as a temporary landing pad and are less interested in learning, or because you decide later on that they aren't the right fit. Such decisions cost you more money in the long run. Investing your time and money in people who truly specialize in the role your company needs will have immense payoffs later.

2. Value each role: With each team member bringing something special to the table, treating each role as an essential part of your operation is also crucial. Each team member should feel like their job matters, without ever asking themselves, 'Why am I even here?'

3. Communicate: The best way to demonstrate value between team members is through communication. It's difficult to feel like you are part of a team when everybody has information that hasn't been shared with you yet or when team members don't fill each other in on what they're working on. Keep a level of transparency whenever possible with all team members, even if the information does not directly pertain to every person on your team.

4. Set goals: Setting short and long-term goals with your team also becomes the foundation for every task they set out to complete each day. Being enthusiastic about the outcome and motivating each other with positive reinforcement will help your team members to make sure that they work with a sense of the big picture, knowing why every task is necessary for achieving a longer-term goal.

5. Celebrate successes and failures: Celebrating your successes and milestones also brings your team together and allows everyone to see that when they work together, great things can happen. If someone does a great job, give them a shout-out in front of the rest of the team so that every effort is seen and appreciated. This also helps each person to feel visible and recognize that what they're doing has an impact. In contrast, if your team fails at something, come together to redirect your efforts or turn it into something positive. Don't throw anyone under the bus or turn a damage-control discussion into a blame game. This never helps anybody. Instead, give your team equal responsibility to put your heads together and figure out the next steps or pivots.

6. Know each other: You are never obligated to become best friends on a personal level with your team members. But having a monthly outing or engaging in some offsite socializing can give team members a chance to appreciate one another for more than just the job they do. Getting to know the people you work with helps you understand their style of work and how to have constructive discussions with them.

These are some basic human resource policies that founders need to inculcate within the organizations as they grow and ensure that they can retain staff. We all know that a new recruit performs productively for a start-up after a few quarters, retaining good talent is key rather than having a culture of hire-fire, which unfortunately few start-ups have, as they feel it reflects the aggressive nature of the entrepreneur.

HIRING IS EASY, RETAINING IS NOT

Finding the right talent is not an easy task in the life of a start-up. A lot of time and energy is spent by the founders in recruiting the key hires and building a team. There are clear lessons to be learnt here for founders from the experiences of other entrepreneurs.

According to Pankit Desai and Anand Naik, the founders of Sequretek, 'Both Anand and I had corporate work experience and hence, we both came from places where structures were already in place.' In reality, things were slightly different.

'What happened was that as we started to build the business, we hired people whom we knew from our earlier companies. We realized later that not everyone can make transition from working in a corporate to a start-up structure. Many a times, you need to bring in the hands-on mode of work into application, many would have done that in their early days but now they could not. We also realized that people need to be mentally prepared to work in scenarios that keep changing. A start-up trajectory is never the same, and it is constantly changing. You need people who can adapt to change. In our case, initially we tested several business models but had to shut them. As founders, you keep trying to make things work and that level of fluidity is not present in everyone,' says Pankit.

He also thinks that as founders their working style is very hands-on. Maybe that did not allow many of the people they hired to flourish. The result was that the churn rate was very high. 'Five years into the business, we have managed to get a hold on the churn rate. And hence, we decided we will not hire people we have already worked with. Finally, I also feel that many people join thinking they are doing the start-up a favour by taking up this job at a pay cut, and on the other hand, we think we are doing you a favour by making you a part of the journey. Clearly that's not how it works,' says Pankit.

'I think as founders we often underplay the importance of recruitment. Today, I spent over 30 per cent of my time on hiring and retaining key personnel,' says Pankit. 'This isn't a role that can be delegated to the HR manager.'

As you bring in new people within a company, a stressful interplay is underway between the new recruits and the old, who have been with the start-up from the early days. And also, between the new recruits and the founding team.

The new recruits who come and build the business from a scale up stage to an enterprise are usually more qualified, have worked in larger organizations and tend to come at higher salaries. The older folks tend to be those who have the implicit trust of the founder, tend to be lesser qualified and with lesser global work experience. However, they are the ones who built the business from the early days to the scale up and know the intricacies of the product, the journey of the company and can move things within the organization as they know all the key decision makers.

So, in any start-up which is on the threshold of becoming an enterprise, not all co-founders are equally involved. There are some co-founders who think their executive role within the organization is diminishing and they don't enjoy their newer roles. While as shareholders, they don't resent the new folks that are joining the company, as executives there is stress between some co-founders and those joining the company at senior executive levels.

Phaneesh had some interesting learnings to share. He was the odd-one out within the company and had started to bring big ticket projects to the company. When asked how he saw his interplay with the company founders as he began to grow within the company, he said: 'It was a huge challenge because by that time, you start to see contribution of different people. And you realize that your worth is nothing compared to theirs. Infosys stock was doing well. So, there was some resentment when I looked at some of the co-founders and older employees. The resentment from my side was that I did the work and a majority of the heavy lifting. There was this perennial question I had for the founders: "You went from zero to $1 million in 10 years and called it stellar performance. Then from $1–1.5 million to $750 million in 10 years and in which I was a part of the success, but am not accorded the same kind of treatment, value, and wealth creation." It was a challenge for me, but I must confess that advice from Mr Murthy and Nandan was helpful. That is when I focused on what was on my plate rather than on somebody else's,' he said.

Given his personal experience, Phaneesh's advice is, 'As your company becomes more valuable you should make sure that you are getting value commensurate with your contribution. I think it's very important to get personal satisfaction. If you think somebody else is taking away the value, then you don't feel good about it. '

That is a key role of a start-up founder as a leader: to retain the old employees and keep them motivated while ensuring the new folks who are taking the company to the next level are also recognized. This is not an easy challenge for a founder to handle and it takes time. Building teams, keeping them motivated and integrating cross sections is one area where I have seen second- or third-time entrepreneurs always do well.

BEING START-UP BATTLE READY

- Recruit people who are smarter and better than you, but have the confidence to be able to manage them.
- Don't get tempted to hire those who are cut from the same cloth; instead choose those who bring in diverse thoughts.
- Hiring is a task the founder himself must drive and cannot be relegated to an HR manager.
- Be careful when you hire from larger companies. Often the most successful executives cannot function in a start-up format.
- While bringing newer members in, it is a challenge not to lose the older members who are the custodians of knowledge and have been loyal to the company.
- Use ESOPs as a key hiring tool but be cautious about it. Most start-ups make mistakes with ESOP allocations that affect the company later.

13

LUCK IS IMPORTANT,
BUT YOU NEED TO STEER IT

One of the most debatable questions in the start-up community, across the globe is, 'Does success come from skill or luck?' Jack Dorsey, founder of Twitter and Square had tweeted in January 2013, 'Success is never accidental.' This is the standard alpha male syndrome among founders who believe their success is not a stroke of luck. However, it is in stark contrast of what other successful entrepreneurs have noted.

Warren Buffet's famous words, when explaining his stroke of luck were that he 'was born a member of the lucky sperm club' and 'winner of the ovarian lottery.' Bezos attributes Amazon's success to an 'incredible planetary alignment' and jokes that it is 'half due to luck, half due to good timing and the rest to his brains.' While Bezos and Buffet might have been trying to put up a humble façade, there is no doubt that luck plays a role in the entrepreneurial journey, just as it does in life.

While writing the success stories of entrepreneurs, we often attribute part of their success to the 'right place, right time' phenomenon. Entrepreneurship is about spotting opportunities. It is all about having a nose for picking trends and getting one's foot in through half open doors. But successful entrepreneurs are not alone in spotting opportunities. They are the ones who upon chancing the opportunity, go ahead with perfect execution to create a successful business.

When someone decides to start a business, they are doing so because there is an opportunity that they believe will satisfy a requirement for both users and consumers (by creating a product or service) and themselves (by being independent, successful and creating wealth and fame). An entrepreneur starts a business only if he/she believes in the existence of an opportunity that is also profitable. That is not luck, it is common sense. But what does matter is timing.

Jonathan Abrams's name is not well known today in the annals of start-up history, but he was indeed the founder of 'social networks'. In 2002, he started Friendster, a social networking platform for friends and was a pared down version of Facebook. Immediately after the launch of Friendster, similar networks were launched. Michael Birch launched Bebo in the UK (acquired and killed by AOL), Google launched Orkut, and Myspace was launched. All these entrepreneurs, including Zuckerberg, had realized that with the open architecture of the internet, with the ubiquitous presence of the broadband and a human desire to communicate and stay in touch, social networks would become a big business. They all understood the virality and power of social networks that was to be unleashed.

However, it was only Zuckerberg who executed it to perfection to create Facebook which now covers 3 billion people in its network, while the others have all died. This was due to his focused, aggressive plan of capturing the easiest market, one step at a time: from Harvard University, Ivy League Universities, East Coast Universities to all US universities and finally to all users with email addresses above the age of 13. Right across, he had the underlying technology to be able to scale up fast and add value added offerings like newsfeed, social graphs, sharing music and other sticky applications.

Being in the right place is key, but execution post that is what ensures success.

LUCK AND COMMON SENSE

Luck does play a role in business, as it does in most walks of life. But when you start talking about luck in entrepreneurship, you can never attribute too much credit to luck for the success of an entrepreneur.

Luck means that a variable is random, and the outcome just happens to be positive purely by chance. Successful entrepreneurs aren't successful because they rolled dice but because they were persistent in their efforts took calculated decisions and had enough motivation to take action at a point in time. It is not about hitting a six and making the ball go out of the boundary of the field but keep the score board ticking by making those singles without getting caught. They saw opportunity, the chance to be and decided to go for it given they had the skills to make it happen. One is not successful because lady luck smiles on them, one's business booms because one is opportunistic at the right time.

Most failed businesses flop because the owner was opportunistic at the wrong time. This is quite common. That is why we say there is no longer any first mover advantage. Sometimes, it helps to not move fast but let the environment settle down and then you make a success of the opportunity.

Entrepreneurs write their own destiny by making choices that lead to actions and those who make the right choices at the right time earn their successes. Entrepreneurs seize moments when they come face to face with a brush of luck. They have a sense of what is good for them. Entrepreneurs are inherently optimists. While the future is unknown, optimists welcome the future while pessimists fear it. Optimists (read entrepreneurs) are looking to change the status quo while pessimists inherently favour status quo and abhor change. Because entrepreneurs are looking to break free from the shackle, they get more opportunities and hence are considered lucky.

Saumil Majmudar, founder of SportzVillage, has an interesting take on luck. Starting up SportzVillage seemed to be the perfect combination as sports was a passion for Saumil and he found a fundamental customer problem to solve. 'For me it was a serendipitous moment when I came up with the idea of SportzVillage. The idea came to my mind when a friend remarked that his six-year-old son spent more time in front of the TV and computer and shied away from participating in any physical activity. That led me to create SportzVillage. Serendipity does not get as much credit as it deserves in the journey of an entrepreneur. Most of the time the big decisions that we take in life has a stroke of serendipity.'

On the other hand, Amod Malviya from Udaan has a different perspective of luck. While acknowledging the fact that he believed in it, he said that 'there are lots of caveats to it. If you think in probabilistic terms, then you cannot have 100 per cent probability in everything. It will be very presumptuous of anybody to think about deterministic result. But you can certainly maximize probability. For e.g. in a start-up, having great people to work with will have a huge impact. But does it mean that if you have the brightest and best minds to work with, you will not fail? In case of Udaan, the implementation of GST gave a great boost to the business and a huge room to grow. Was that a stroke of luck? The more we accept that there are many factors that are not controlled by us and thereby no deterministic outcome, the more we expose ourselves to variability. I believe in probabilistic outcome than luck.'

Acknowledging the role luck plays in one's careers would oblige one to accept that we have less control over what happens in our lives than most of us want to admit. We commonly come across three kinds of luck: circumstantial, constitutional and dumb luck. Although you cannot alter the latter, I strongly believe you can work toward creating or strengthening the first two.

THE THREE KINDS OF LUCK

Circumstantial luck occurs when you are flying with a friend who bumps into a third person, who then ends up becoming one of your most important clients. None of this would have happened if you had not chosen that particular lunch-date or restaurant, or if that third party hadn't shown up at just the right moment.

Sometimes an individual's age, cultural background, nationality and upbringing help predispose them to a certain outcome. When that happens, it's called constitutional luck. For instance, even attending the same college or university can help a person out. The business world can be insular and clannish, and the fortuitous similarity of a specific hereditary or cultural background can be useful while making connections. There is no doubt that this helps, as you see the number of unicorns in India who have graduated from IITs/IIMs and other premier institutes.

Age can certainly make a difference, too. Consider all those digitally savvy millennials who were born into digital consumption and who profited from an industry that matched up well with their talents, ambitions and visions. That way, even our generation was lucky as we began our professional lives as India was opening up and the entire gold-rush was there to be a part of the 'New India'.

Finally, there is plain dumb luck where you win the lottery.

HOW IS IT THAT ENTREPRENEURS MAKE THEMSELVES LUCKY?

First, be humble, it does pay. Bill Gates famously said: 'Success is a lousy teacher. It seduces smart people into thinking they can't lose.' Always remember, no matter how powerful and successful an entrepreneur becomes, they need to retain a measure of humility. Acknowledging your own vulnerability is not a sign of weakness but sometimes it miraculously summons those individuals who can help you achieve your goals.

All of us have had chance encounters; entrepreneurs are humble enough to believe that in some cases, they must seize these encounters as they happen, because the world won't easily offer up such opportunities again. It is the outgoing nature, perennial drive and optimistic attitude that enables them to capture the chance encounter.

Second, successful founders tend to have a high degree of intellectual curiosity. They usually are genuinely interested in the lives of others. The constant desire to improve themselves and their business makes them mix with people who they think will add value to their lives.

It is this trait of curiosity that allows entrepreneurs to think out-of-the-box and come up with solutions to problems that have not been solved yet. It also allows them to be engaged with the world around them and ask relevant questions. Sometimes, it is curiosity that allows an entrepreneur to spot an opportunity.

Third, and most importantly, as mentioned above, entrepreneurs have an optimistic attitude—one of belief in opportunity.

Maturity dawns on everyone with the passage of time. I didn't believe in timing. For me it was simple: if I am working hard, I will succeed; no external force can change that. This was the youthful mojo in me. I still believe hard work always brings rewards, but with a sprinkling of luck or coincidence, reaching the goal becomes that much faster.

With time, I have realized that all of us must go through rough patches. Alongside the purple ones. It is akin to the 'bad patch' even Sachin Tendulkar fell into in when he was aiming for his 100th ton. It took him 11 months and 27 innings to get to the landmark. During that period, no matter what he did, he could not achieve the target. He had come tantalizingly close a few times.

Luck is just a small part of the entrepreneur's journey. As an entrepreneur, you are going to be challenged every single day by problems at work. There will be times in the journey when your chips are down. During these times, however hard you try, you will encounter failures. A weak entrepreneur gets caught up in this and begins to doubt themselves. At such moments, it is important to be aware of your state of mind and stay in control of your energy levels. You may have to change your normal style of functioning to survive these times.

A few of the simple things I practice when I fall into such times are:

- **Don't try too hard:** I stay optimistic and get into a mindset to believe in myself. During such times, I don't over try, as I believe that pushing hard against a wall is futile. You have to wait for the time a crack appears in the wall, to be able to push it.
- **Stop blaming myself:** Earlier, I would blame myself and would ruminate the past actions that had brought me to the state. I realized that this was a downward spiral. The way I react now is to avoid overthinking and stop blaming myself.
- **Make the attitude adjustment and remain optimistic:** People cannot stop themselves from thinking about one thing or the other. However, now I work hard to control what I think about, so when my thoughts start wavering towards a negative space, I consciously focus on reshuffling them to something more positive. Negative thoughts can bog one down and are self-perpetuating. If you decide to ignore the negative thoughts and focus on what's important, you kill them before they grow bigger in your head.
- **Slow down:** I consciously get out of my overdrive. When chips

are down, many entrepreneurs tend to do more, hoping something will create a change of luck and scenario. On the contrary, because of the confused state the mind is in, this leads to greater chaos and one digs a deeper hole. It is best to take a step back and relax.

- **Be aware:** Leadership is all about awareness of situation and alertness. Knowing the state of your business is going to help you react to the situation appropriately. It will give you confidence to take decisions more proactively.

Abhinay Choudhari is a firm believer in luck: 'Of course luck has its part to play. In the last round of funding that we raised, I think getting Alibaba, at the last minute, was due to luck. We were in talks with two other players and for some reason they backed out, and Alibaba came in. If we would have signed with either of the other funds, our world would have been very different.'

Lou Holtz, former American football player, coach and analyst, had a great quote, 'Life is 10 per cent of what happens to you and 90 per cent of how you deal with it.' People who consider themselves unlucky and constantly blame their luck for failures, are those who do not believe in this maxim. Successful entrepreneurs are those who are inherent optimists and always find a silver lining in the darkest clouds. They look inwards for reasons and try to adapt positively to situations that might otherwise seem negative.

BEING START-UP BATTLE READY

- Being in the 'right place at the right time' does not ensure success; one has to capitalize on it.
- Make the most of serendipitous opportunities.
- With time, one understands to maximize results when the tailwinds and luck are behind you.
- When there is a strong series of bad luck and nothing seems to work, it is better to just lie low and survive the times.
- Don't be hard on yourself and have self-doubt when things are not going for you.
- Don't blame luck for failures and mistakes. Only pessimists do that and all entrepreneurs need to be optimists in their thinking and approach.

14

INTRAPRENEURSHIP: MERELY A JOB OR A FULCRUM OF INNOVATION?

As a start-up grows and passes through the consolidation phase, one of the biggest challenges is to have enterprise-level systems in place, but still retain the start-up culture of nimbleness, lean thinking, innovation, business-pivoting and always questioning the status quo.

A number of companies fall into a moribund state and lumber along after the initial years of entrepreneurial drive. This often frustrates the founder who can't make changes anymore within the organizational structure and board, and leaves the business to a professional CEO who resembles a maintenance manager more than an innovator. This is the oft-repeated story of most start-ups which scale to become enterprises.

Yet, how is it that Apple, Google and other Silicon Valley organizations are not merely scaling up their core business but constantly innovating and launching not just newer products, but newer adjunct lines of businesses. What makes these organizations different from the myriad other well-funded scaled-up start-ups who get into the maintenance mode of working merely on the quarterly financials for their investors. It is because these companies have kept the 'DNA of entrepreneurship' integral to the company, despite their size and scale.

In the mid-'80s, Jobs and a team of 20 Apple engineers split off to develop the Apple Macintosh computer, or 'Mac' for short. This group could operate independently or 'without adult supervision', as per the folklore of Apple. This band of creative, innovative and entrepreneurial employees effectively created competition for Apple's main line of products.

The history of Post-Its' discovery is well documented in the annals of innovation history. Simple and effective, the Post-it Note is a key part of any desk stationery. 3M scientist Spencer Silver's invention—an adhesive that stuck lightly to surfaces—went without use for years until Art Fry, a fellow 3M employee, was searching for a way to keep bookmarks from falling out of his books.

Employees at Google are allowed time for personal projects. Some of Google's best projects come out of their 20 per cent time policy. One of these was Gmail, launched on 1 April 2004.

Ken Kutaragi, a relatively junior Sony Employee, spent hours tinkering with his daughter's Nintendo to make it more powerful and user friendly. What came from his work turned into one of the world's most recognizable brands—the Sony PlayStation.

INTRAPRENEURS ARE THE DREAMERS WHO DO

These organizations inculcate a spirit of 'intrapreneurship.' An intrapreneur, as defined by the Cambridge Dictionary, is 'an employee who takes direct responsibility for turning an idea into a new product or service. An intrapreneur brings entrepreneurial thinking and skills to build within the structure of an existing organization.'

The concept of intrapreneurship is credited to Gifford Pinchot, an American entrepreneur, author and inventor, who coined the term in a paper he co-wrote with his wife in 1978, entitled 'Intra-Corporate Entrepreneurship'. Pinchot highlights that, while intrapreneurs possess qualities such as intrinsic motivation and responsibility, they also display what he describes as the 'both' characteristic. That is to say, intrapreneurship is more than just being an 'ideas factory'; real intrapreneurship means taking responsibility for the management of that idea and seeing it through to profitable reality, or as Pinchot puts it so succinctly in his 1985 book *Intrapreneuring*,[15] 'Intrapreneurs are the dreamers who do'.

---

[15]Gifford Pinchot. *Intrapreneuring*. Harper & Row, 1985.

One of the most entrepreneurial organizations at present is the Virgin group. The behemoth reflects the entrepreneurial spirit of its founder Richard Branson. 'Intrapreneurs are employees who do for corporate innovation what an entrepreneur does for his or her start-up,' is another definition that Branson uses. 'Intrapreneurship is nothing new,' Richard Branson believes, 'a title hasn't gotten nearly the amount of attention it deserves is entrepreneur's little brother, intrapreneur.'

He or she is an employee who is given financial support and autonomy to create new products, services and systems for the benefit of the company. While it's true that every company needs an entrepreneur to get it underway, healthy growth requires a smattering of intrapreneurs who drive new projects, and explore new and unexpected directions for business development.

Sameer Garde, President India and SAARC at Cisco India, has worked with top MNCs in India but has been a quintessential intrapreneur. He is a firm believer than intrapreneurs can thrive at large organizations. 'In fact, most of the successful leaders are the one who challenged the status quo and tried to do their own thing. So yes, intrapreneurship can survive in a corporate. It does become a challenge sometimes because of the structures and frameworks in large organizations. In my professional journey so far, every time someone has said something was a bad idea, it has made me instinctively think that it's a good idea,' he says.

Sameer also shared that there is not much difference between an entrepreneur and an intrapreneur, for instance, both have to take risk and sometimes some bets taken will fail. 'It was the early '90s and I was working with a leading durable appliance company, and India had still not understood the meaning of high double-digit growth. I was given the mandate of Maharashtra for sales. And in one of the meetings, I was told they needed to grow by 4.5 per cent. I realized that Maharashtra is a vast region and to get optimum coverage, I decided to break it into smaller areas and within 1.5 years our Compound Annual Growth Rate (CAGR) was 29–30 per cent. But after a few years, when I re-joined the same company and tried to do something similar it didn't work out. So, like entrepreneurs, intrapreneurs also take risks—sometimes they work and sometimes they do not,' says Sameer.

He also makes a valid point when he says that a lot also depends on the company and culture it has. 'I have never been seen as someone who will collaborate on everything that is said or do what has been told. Sometimes that may work against you. I have worked with a whole range of MNCs including Dell, Philips and now Cisco, and each of these organizations has helped me grow too. For instance, at Dell, where I spent 10 years, they have a simple principle, your suggestion or solution for any problem should be direct and to the point. There is no point in giving long responses and no end to it. I get extremely frustrated when I see hours and hours being spent in meetings and people, who instead of coming to the point, continue explaining. There are very few organizations that allow you to work in an absolutely no control framework. Philips is one such organization that does not believe in unnecessary control. At Cisco, there are people doing some really crazy stuff in their own small vertical or segment and I may come to know of it later, but that independence is there,' he told me.

While entrepreneurs start up and run their own companies, intrapreneurs are responsible for innovating within an existing organization. The setting is not the only difference between the terms. Another important differentiator is risk. Working within an established business, intrapreneurs are arguably taking less risks than those leading ventures of their own.

The flip side is that entrepreneurship offers more freedom, unrestricted by the operations of an existing organization and the possible limitations that come with that, while also standing to gain the most if the venture is successful.

Given these definitions, it is fair to say that intrapreneurship is considered highly beneficial for both the intrapreneur and the organization they are operating within. From the point of view of the organization, fostering intrapreneurship can result in innovative change, results and an increased agility that, at the most basic level, improve efficiency, reduce costs or increase profitability.

It helps businesses generate growth and adds a level of flexibility; while a company may have become very strong in a particular area, an intrapreneur might find a new and different opportunity, direction or way of working.

Intrapreneurship also has the benefit of opening an organization's eyes to potential leaders of projects. Intrapreneurs think and act differently than other employees and possess characteristics often considered desirable in senior management. Engaging these employees in different company functions has the dual benefit of helping a company identify future leaders and training them at the same time.

Some of the frustrations that plague the founder in his journey of growth happen during the consolidation phase when he realizes the start-up which he had built to reflect his thinking and DNA, now has its own character and some aspects he doesn't like. When the business succeeds, complacency and arrogance creep in with the leadership team. The structure becomes an unwieldy and bureaucratic, stifling initiative. The reward system doesn't encourage people to put their head above the parapet and there is no incentive for innovation. The driver is maintenance management and short-term quarter-on-quarter thinking, discouraging any longer-term strategic thinking or risk taking.

Often, the entrepreneur, frustrated with the state of the business, either leaves the organization or decides to break through the structure and shake it at its roots. Subhash Chandra, the founder and chairman of the Zee Networks, was a proponent of this method. He felt that every organization needs a shakeup and reinvigoration from time to time to break the shackles of bureaucracy. Every four or five years, he would take charge of the business and try to awaken the start-up culture within the organization again.

To create intrapreneurs within an organization, the company must:

- Be attentive and encourage initiative.
- Give employees ownership of projects.
- Make risk-taking and failure acceptable.
- Train employees in innovation.
- Give employees time outside their core job definition.
- Encourage networking and collaboration.
- Create a knowledge-based organization.
- Reward new ideas.

One of the most celebrated intrapreneurs of our times is Phaneesh Murthy, who built the sales team and structure at Infosys. He was one of the senior hires at Infosys and was mandated to build the marketing and sales team, and branding for the company. The founders of Infosys gave him aircover and created an environment for him to excel.

Says Phaneesh, 'The first few months when I came to the US were very difficult. Those were the days when we used to make cold calls. You didn't have email. There were days on days when I hadn't talked to another human. I would just keep recording messages on voice mail. It was all self-motivated.'

His close observation also helped him to suggest business decisions to the founders, which would differentiate Infosys from the crowd. At iGATE too, though he was the CEO, he ran the operations of the company like an entrepreneur, with a clear understanding with the founders to not interfere in the day-to-day operations.

At Infosys, when Phaneesh proposed the creation of a brand, many within the company were taken by surprise because branding was associated with fast-moving consumer goods (FMCG) players at the time. 'Fortunately, Mr Murthy and Nandan were convinced,' says Phaneesh. I think, as an intrapreneur, he managed to convince everyone in the company to create something which hadn't been done before.

As an entrepreneur, one needs to understand the signals that your customer is sending and make changes to your organization, product and services to better cater to their concerns. Phaneesh shared that this was what Infosys excelled at. 'After we were selected by GE for an alliance, Nortel too followed suit. But they said that they would pay much higher than the rate prevalent then because they did not want us to be sweat shops and would use the profits to build a long-term infrastructure they could use. They wanted India to have world-class infrastructure. That was the defining moment for the industry that saw the birth of dedicated offshore centres,' reminiscences Phaneesh.

Another instance Phaneesh shared was that of his contract negotiation with GE. There are a few clauses within a contract that never get negotiated. One of them is the force majeure clause. 'The clause basically said that if there was a natural calamity, fire or riots, then you were waived off from your delivery responsibility. GE was the first company to change this clause, and they said they only wanted to do business with people who could support them even if there was an earthquake in one part of the city. That is the birth of multi-city centres, with hot site backup and redundancy,' said Phaneesh.

The free hand given to him by the founders of Infosys stood in great stead for Phaneesh when he began his entrepreneurial journey.

His entrepreneurial bet Quintant Services, which raised $30 million from investors was based on the feedback he got from customers when he was with Infosys. The outcome-based model which the industry now uses had its first seller in Quintant, which was soon acquired by iGATE.

Phaneesh's story is an interesting one of an intrapreneur par excellence who flourished within the enterprise and used the same skills and knowledge to bring forth a change within an industry and create another successful business venture.

So is the case with Sudip Bandyopadhyay as well. Prior to acquiring the listed company JRG Securities and rebranding it as Inditrade as founder and executive chairman, he was a senior executive responsible for starting the financial services for Reliance ADAG. He admits, 'My stint in Reliance helped me in growing this venture. When I joined Reliance, they didn't have any financial services. I was the first hire; they had the built the mutual fund side but nothing on the financial side. Right from applying for incorporating a company, bidding for BSE card, acquiring a life insurance business, etc. everything was done by me. Even if I wanted a secretary, I had to hire one myself. I suppose my first entrepreneurial gig started with Reliance, although I was within the corporate framework of a large entity.'

◆

Interfaced closely with the concept of intrapreneurship is the concept of corporate venturing.

Corporate venturing is the concept of large enterprises either developing, sponsoring or investing in start-up companies in order to develop innovative products or services. This offers recognition within the large enterprises that need to deal closely with the start-up world, as innovation will not happen within the enterprise's core organizational structures.

Typically, corporate venturing takes place within the core industry the corporation operates in. An energy giant such as BP is likely to back energy tech ventures via its corporate venturing unit, while a large pharmaceutical firm Astra Zeneca would concentrate their venturing efforts in the pharma and healthcare sectors. However, some corporate venturing units will operate like VC firms, investing in opportunities where they can add value regardless of the industry.

While there is considerable overlap between corporate venturing and R&D in terms of product development, the key differentiation is that corporate venturing will typically involve a separate 'start-up' company, funded by the corporate parent. The advantages of this approach include more freedom for the start-up to operate without corporate bureaucracy and the opportunity to also become a self-sustaining business in its own right—not just selling the product or service to the corporate parent, but also to other firms, even sometimes to the competition. However, it is not without controversy, and a key challenge has been fostering collaboration between corporate venturing and R&D departments without either group feeling marginalized.

For an entrepreneur, corporate venturing provides access to resources and markets. This is particularly important in deep domain sectors such as energy, medical diagnostics, spacetech and deep tech where a small number of large players dominate the market, so partnering with them enables instant access to a customer base. Additionally, if an entrepreneur has successfully developed a business and secured VC funding, corporate venturing units provide an effective exit for both the founder and the VC investor. The corporate venturing unit can take a successful start-up in their relevant industry and integrate it into their core business, achieving the economies of scale needed for future growth.

Sameer is now part of an organization which had been an early proponent of corporate venture. 'I think there is a heightened sense of awareness about entrepreneurship within companies now, compared to a decade ago. Within Cisco too, we have supported employees who have shown this zeal. Recently, two of our employees were given seed funding for a project they were working on and now they have hived off and started as a company. Rather, John Chambers would prefer that if employees have the potential to innovate and build, and many a times would also acquire them,' said Sameer.

The venture arms of tech firms have been investing in start-ups for quite some time now. There are a few factors to bear in mind: traditionally, tech firms have always had plenty of cash on books and when it comes to allocating it, investing in the start-up segment makes sense. The other factor is the pace of innovation. The pace at which innovation happens in a start-up is difficult for a large corporate to maintain. Unlike innovation earlier, where you were creating a large network setup, now it's about innovation in micro segments but their impact is huge. Sameer highlights this point, 'For instance, we recently acquired 42hertz, which looks like a small firm, but the niche space that it occupies will have a huge impact on our collaboration suits. It is not that Cisco could not have done this in-house, but the time taken for an MVP and then getting clearances is significantly greater for large firms.'

BEING START-UP BATTLE READY

- A founder must strive to keep the start-up entrepreneurial and innovative, and not get caught in the web of bureaucracy.
- Employees must be given a degree of freedom and aircover to make mistakes for the organization to be innovative.
- The rewards system must be designed to accommodate innovation and out-of-the-box thinking.
- Intrapreneurial experiences stand in great stead when one begins their entrepreneurial journey and helps to make the most of it.
- Successful companies encourage intrapreneurs and try to retain talent who will fast outgrow their roles.

15

THIS IS MY LIFE, CAN THERE BE A LIFE BEYOND THIS?

What does it mean for founders when they say they want to step back? A step back can be one of several things. It might mean being less involved in the day-to-day decision-making of the company and taking more of a strategic outlook concerning the company's future and empowering others to make decisions.

For others, it might mean stepping away completely and hiring someone else as CEO to run the company. This is sometimes voluntary, as founders understand that it's the best choice for the business. However, it can also be a point of contention in certain situations, with investors demanding new leadership, either to bring someone new in or promote someone internally.

In 2019, the founders of Google, Larry Page and Sergey Brin, announced that they were relinquishing their roles at Google's parent company Alphabet and were stepping away from the management for good, but that they would remain on the board. Sundar Pichai, CEO of Google, is now managing Alphabet too. Though this transition had surprised many, it had been evident as both the founders had already reduced their interaction within the company.

However, if one remembers Google's story, they will know there was also a time when the founders had been asked by the board to relinquish their CEO title.

In 2001, Larry Page was forced to relinquish his role as CEO to Eric

Schmidt of Novell. The move came after the high-profile attempt by Page to fire all project managers Google had employed at the time. One of the other reasons was that the fast-growing company was becoming too much to handle for the young founders. So, at the behest of the investors, Eric Schmidt was roped in, as Sergey Brin had then famously said, for 'parental supervision'.

Schmidt did a wonderful job at Google and took it to public markets in 2004 at a valuation of $27 billion. In 2011, after being at the helm of the company for a decade, Schmidt moved on to the role of executive chairman and Larry Page was given the reins of the CEO again. The move then, predicted many tech analysts, was to shake Google from being just a web-focused company. True to the vision of the founders—Page and Brin—Google in the next four years got into technology space such as driverless cars, AI, cloud, Nexus Smartphones, quantum computing, etc.

In 2015, in order to bring more clarity and accountability within the company, the founders created a new company called Alphabet, and announced Sundar Pichai as the CEO of Google, who would report to the board. But this was a much more mature transition and with a clear mandate that the founders wanted to get out of the everyday operational issues of the company, and gave the steering wheel of Google to Pichai. In December 2019, Page and Brin announced they were handing over the management of Alphabet to Sundar Pichai: 'Sundar brings humility and a deep passion for technology to our users, partners and our employees every day. He's worked closely with us for 15 years, through the formation of Alphabet, as CEO of Google, and a member of the Alphabet Board of Directors. He shares our confidence in the value of the Alphabet structure, and the ability it provides us to tackle big challenges through technology. There is no one that we have relied on more since Alphabet was founded, and no better person to lead Google and Alphabet into the future.'

FOUNDER'S DILEMMA: STEP DOWN AS FOUNDER CEO

A founder gives his blood, toil, sweat and tears to transform an idea into a company of scale. They establish the start-up from its fledgling foundations into a stage of maturity. During the journey, stepping down and looking beyond the company seems to be the furthest from their mind.

But, during the journey it behooves the question, 'When is the right time to let someone else captain the ship?' There is no right answer in this regard. It can be a voluntary decision of the founder who works towards ensuring his successor is in place for a smooth transition, or can be decided by the investors who feel that the founder has passed his sell-by-date and that the growth of the company calls for a new leader.

Most founders not only aspire to create and run the next breakthrough business, but also hope to stay with the start-up throughout the company's growth cycle, such as Jeff Bezos and Mark Zuckerberg, the world's poster children for tremendous, long-term entrepreneurial success. However, these titans are the exception rather than the rule, as the skills needed to start a business and grow it to a certain level, and then to expand it to a very large company, are very different. The skills at each stage vary, and it takes considerable strength to realize that you might not be the best person to move forward at the helm later on in the company's life.

Founders realize that post subsequent rounds of funding, there is a need for aggressive growth that may require a CEO with experience, someone with a demonstrable record of running a successful high-growth business. This decision of the founder begins with self-introspection about the right person who can take the company to its next stage.

The critical issue is, a founder's hostility to change is simply down to their inability to let go and understand that they are no longer the right person for the job. Passion and dedication are integral for a founder to take the first leap of faith to build a start-up, but when it comes to implementing large internal structures (those that allow a business to run smoothly), that very approach and attitude can cause significant and sometimes fatal problems for companies that are trying to transition.

In the early days of a start-up, founders are often busy firefighting and excel in dousing these fires swiftly, but later on the goal is fire prevention. Natural biases can cause one to view circumstances through rose-tinted glasses, causing an overestimation of one's own ideas, ability, knowledge and chances of success. Similarly, one might underestimate competitors, lack the understanding of resource requirements and fail to foresee and plan for emergencies. Reluctance to hand over day-to-day control of the child the founder has nurtured and raised is undoubtedly a difficult step, but more often than not, a necessary one.

A start-up's growth is strongly connected to the founder, who is usually very hands-on and clued-in on all that is happening. Their leadership is at the heart of decision-making and integrating the various pieces of the business model. It is hard work, involves long hours and their touch can be felt across the entire business. The role relies on a deep appreciation of the industry and the start-up's vision and opportunity. Business operations are adaptable and dynamic when the start-up is learning how real-world complications affect the business

Under such circumstances, hiring a CEO is both high stakes and risk, but it has the potential to have a transformative effect in catapulting the company to the next level of growth.

As the business stabilizes, the product roadmap becomes stronger, technology matures, revenues increase and the next stage of planning for growth and expansion begins. This also signals another phase of evolution into new product or service lines, or even an acceptance to exit.

This phase is crucial and different from what the entrepreneur has been doing so far. The growth in this phase demands consistent integration, coordination and sharing of leadership with a wider senior team. The CEO must be sensitive to the people they are responsible for—shareholders, consumers and employees.

It is here that the roles diverge, the founder cannot be involved in every single decision, leaving the day-to-day decision-making to the senior team instead and acting more as a conductor. They become more of a figurehead and statesman/stateswoman, guiding and developing ideas while promoting the business.

Thus, the CEO is now required to turn their hands to selling, marketing, support, finance and legal problems. These aren't always the skills that a successful early-stage founder is equipped with, or perhaps the start-up is moving too fast for the founder to have the necessary time to develop them.

THE EXIT

Once the decision for the founder's exit has been made, the next step is working out when the transition should take place, to avoid the costly error of doing it too early or too late. This is a make-or-break situation in the life of a company. There are innumerable examples of the founders taking a step back to bring in CEOs and the experiment not working, which entails the founder's return. Such a roller-coaster ride takes the company back by a few years.

One such CEO is Howard Schultz of Starbucks. Under his leadership, the company grew from having fewer than 20 stores to more than 100, in four years. In 1992, he took the company public and by the end of the decade, Starbucks had close to 2,500 locations in about a dozen countries. He stepped down in 2000 and became chairman. However, he came back as CEO in 2008, as the company, which by then had a presence in 15,000 locations across the world, was slumping in performance.

When he returned as CEO, Starbucks stock value had fallen by 75 per cent over the previous two years and competition from McDonald's and Dunkin Donuts was eating into sales performance. He decided to close 900 stores and created a blueprint for the company to secure new avenues of growth. By 2012, Starbucks had rebounded.

As a rule of thumb, six months of initiating and managing transition time is key. The board and the senior management must be taken into confidence on this and all must back the 'experiment'. The following important details can ensure a smooth transition:

1. Define the start-up's culture and core values.
2. Select the CEO for leadership, interpersonal skills and experience in creating a supportive culture of collaboration.
3. Facilitate close relationships between the founder, the new CEO and the team.
4. Transfer knowledge.
5. Minimize the handover period.
6. Determine the strategic significance of the transition and keep communication channels accessible.

The relationship between the founder and newly inducted CEO is a complex one. There should be mutual respect and space for the new relationship and structure to succeed and enhance the company value. There will be pressure points, but they must work together, alongside the executive team and the board, to ensure success.

The founder must be able to accept the following:

- Acknowledge and respect that the new CEO will come with experience and will likely do things differently.
- Accept that some decision-making will take longer. CEOs are groomed in a corporate domain where decision-making is methodical and strategic, unlike founders who are generally opportunistic and prone to rely on instinct.
- Empower the CEO to make their own decisions and not undermine them.
- Redirect employees who try to go around the CEO.

In a similar fashion, the new CEO must agree to the following:

- Respect the founder, their strengths, and what they have built.
- To appreciate entrepreneurial procedures while introducing best practice skills and experiences.
- Be a cultural fit with the company and embody the same values as the founder.
- Put the company's best interests first.
- Assure the founder that they are acting in the start-up's best interest.
- Allow the founder to continue to take centre stage at public-facing events.
- Have complementary skills to the founder if they continue to hold a position within the business.

As demonstrated, stepping down and hiring a new CEO is a tough and emotive decision which is both high in stakes and risk. Because at some point, the demands of your role as a founder are likely to exceed your business acumen and skills, and the cost of hiring or managing the process poorly could be drastically detrimental to your company.

However, it has the potential to have a transformative effect in catapulting your company to the next level of growth. By following best practices for when and how to transition founder leadership to growth leadership, it puts you in a far stronger position to manage it successfully

Phaneesh Murthy tells of his induction as CEO of iGATE, at the insistence of Ashok Trivedi, one of the founders of the business. By the time Phaneesh joined iGATE, the company had seen a lot of churn at the CEO level and was desperately in need of an overhaul. Before joining iGATE, Phaneesh had started his own venture Quintant and had raised $30 million from investors.

According to Phaneesh, 'iGATE was listed on the Nasdaq with $65 million as its market cap. It was a poorly managed and a loss-making company. I told him (Ashok) I had my company and that if he wanted me to work for him, then he needed to buy me out, and he agreed. That's how I got into the company. At that time, iGATE's operating margins were minus 20 per cent. I got the most phenomenal experience of my life by converting the company to a plus 25 per cent operating margins in the next few years. I had a great stint at iGATE and used the platform to scale the business and eventually acquire Patni Computer Systems to create a $1 billion business. It was a truly entrepreneurial journey as I killed almost all the business they had and built it from scratch. But I must complement the founders of iGATE as they had realized that as founders, they were unable to scale the business beyond a certain point and they brought me in to change the direction and scale of the business.'

THE LIFE AFTER

The entrepreneur/founder needs to be able to chalk out the path for themselves, to be able to leave the business without harming it.

There are several options for founders once they have stepped down, but the majority of founders stay on to become directors of the businesses. Other succession paths include taking on another role that reports directly to the new CEO or moving on entirely to something different.

Should they work on another start-up? Will they turn into investors as they have the expertise to build businesses? Will they look ahead into social enterprise? Will they join politics? Will they look forward to advisory roles and play golf? Will they now write a book? Will they aim to lead a multi-dimensional life and do all the above? These decisions must be made in the mind of the entrepreneur for them to be able to take a view of their ongoing relationship with the company they founded.

Founders are usually convinced that only they can lead their start-ups to success. 'I'm the one with the vision and the desire to build a great company. No one can take my place,' is a common thought among founders. There is a great deal of truth to that view.

Anu Acharya, the CEO and founder of MapMyGenome and who has had a successful venture, Ocimum, agreed with this. She shared her own experience as a first-time entrepreneur. 'I was very emotional with Ocimum. So, if anyone would ask me even a simple question like, "What valuation do you expect?" I would get very emotional and think how can one place a value to something you start on your own. Also, when they asked if I would sell the business, I would get very emotional,' she reminiscences.

But now she is a much-seasoned entrepreneur. 'Having lived a full cycle of a start-up, I am a mature person and if a situation comes along where my investors ask me to move on and hire a professional CEO, I would be fine with it, given the new CEO can run the company better and increase shareholder value,' she said.

New ventures are usually labors of love for entrepreneurs, and they become emotionally attached to them, referring to the business as their 'baby' and using similar parenting language without even noticing. Their attachment is evident in the relatively low salaries they pay themselves.

Many entrepreneurs are overconfident about their prospects and naive about the problems they will face. Most founder-CEOs start out wanting both wealth and power. However, once they grasp that they'll probably have to maximize one or the other, they will be in a position to figure out which is more important to them. Their past decisions regarding co-founders, hires, and investors will usually tell them which they truly favor. Once they know, they will find it easier to tackle transitions.

Founders who understand that they are motivated more by wealth than by control will themselves bring in new CEOs. By contrast, founders who understand that they are motivated by control are more prone to making decisions that enable them to lead the business at the expense of increasing its value. They are more likely to remain sole founders, use their own capital instead of taking money from investors, resist deals that affect their management control and attract executives who will not threaten their desire to run the company.

I am aware of a technology venture based in Mumbai that wanted to raise $5 million in the first round of financing. During negotiations with potential investors, the founder realized that they were insisting on bringing in a professional CEO. The founder was sure that he was not going to hand the company over to someone else. As a result, he raised only $2 million from another investor, and he remained CEO for the next two years. Founders motivated by control will make decisions that enable them to lead the business at the expense of increasing its value.

One factor that affects the founder's choices is the perception of a venture's potential. Founders often make different decisions when they believe their start-ups have the potential to grow into extremely valuable companies than when they believe their ventures won't be that valuable.

Venture capitalists implicitly use the trade-off between money and control to judge whether they should invest in founder-led companies. A few take it to the extreme by refusing to back founders who aren't motivated by money. Others invest in a start-up only when they're confident the founder has the skills to lead it in the long term. Even these firms have to replace as many as a quarter of the founder-CEOs in the companies they fund.

Heads of not-for-profit organizations must make similar choices. Venkat Krishnan left his successful corporate life to start 'GiveIndia', an organization dedicated to promoting and enabling a culture of 'giving', in 2000. GiveIndia was structured as a philanthropic exchange. His idea was that just as a stock exchange connects companies with investors, GiveIndia would connect worthwhile and credible NGOs to donors. He played an active role in scaling the business and enacting his vision. He got corporate sponsors on board, grew the business and invested in terms of IT, sales and distribution and had a strategic partnership with ICICI. But he was clear that he was becoming an impediment to growth of the idea and was certain he would need to move out. He came up with the idea of Daan Utsav, which was an extension of the GiveIndia movement. He left the GiveIndia role as CEO and handed it over to Dhaval Udani, his alum from IIM Ahmedabad.

Says Venkat, 'I realized that my vision was constricting the growth of the GiveIndia movement. We needed to take it to the next step and that for me was important, as this was a nation-building movement and something that would change the face of giving and philanthropy in India. For me, this was not a peg I wanted to hang my coat on. I therefore moved on and let Dhaval take over the reins of the business to be able to scale the business. Today, GiveIndia is a professionally run organization with CEO Atul Satija and a professional board. Looking back, this was the right direction for the movement.'

Founder of Persistent Systems Anand Deshpande's view on the shift of founder from CEO to another role is interesting. The company had appointed a CEO in 2019 who left after a stint of one-and-a-half years.

'The transition happens because of several things like your age or what you want to do further. I have handled this business for 30 years, day in and day out, and now I am in a situation where I am think I can achieve a lot more as an individual and for some of the tasks I was doing every day, I can hire people. A CEO's job involves a lot of running around; you have to be constantly chasing something or the other and after some time you burn out. So, two years ago there was this pressure on us to separate the chairman and MD office, and I wanted to see how things would work if I moved to the chairman's role and got a CEO. So, we did try and hire someone but he left, and I am still not CEO. We do not have one. I have a team now that runs the day-to-day business. I am still very active in the business and also own 30 per cent of the company shares,' he added.

Anand did agree that it is difficult for a founder to transition to another role. 'It is not an easy transition but then I go back to what I said: you have to do what is right for the company. Moreover, at a certain point in time, you will reach a situation where you are not contributing as well to the company as someone else can. At that point you should find a CEO. And if you can separate ownership from the management, then you can be with the company. Otherwise, you can sell off,' he points out.

There have been instances where, after bringing in professional CEOs, founders have been called back by the shareholders because the CEO failed to deliver. The case of Steve Jobs being booted out of Apple and then returning to take Apple to immense heights is well known. Similar cases are those of Howard Schultz in Starbucks and Tom Singh of Nu Look in London.

Choosing between money, legacy, impact and power allows entrepreneurs to come to grips with what success means to them. Founders who want to manage empires will not believe they are successes if they lose control, even if they end up rich. Conversely, founders who understand that their goal is to amass wealth or leave behind a legacy will not view themselves as failures when they step down from the top job.

Once they realize why they are turning entrepreneur, founders must, as the old Chinese proverb says, 'Decide on three things at the start: the rules of the game, the stakes and the quitting time.'

BEING START-UP BATTLE READY

- A founder must be ready to relinquish the CEO position for the company to grow beyond his limitations.
- A true founder looks to create wealth and leave a legacy rather than to maintain control.
- Bringing in a new CEO of the business is a difficult task for the founder, but he must be responsible for embedding the CEO within the business, else he will never succeed.
- Founders must clearly think through the life beyond the start-up to enable this transition successfully.
- Founders must also be prepared to take charge of the company again, should the board and shareholders feel the need for the same again, after the CEO experiment fails.

16

THE BOILING WATER DIDN'T KILL THE FROG, MISTIMING THE EXIT DID

We are all familiar with the old fable about the frog in a pot of boiling water. The frog was alive when someone put him into a nice, cool pot of water. Then when the pot was put on the stove, the frog was reassured and did not think much of what was going on. When the person turned on the stove, the frog did not notice much difference in the water's temperature until it was too late and it had boiled to death.

What had happened? Apparently with small adjustments in temperature, as the water got hotter and hotter, it got so hot it began boiling. Because of the frog's ability to adapt, it did not realize that the water had reached such a hot temperature that it became impossible to survive. The frog died from the heat even though it could have jumped out of the pot earlier at any time and saved itself. In truth, it was not the boiling water that killed the frog but the wrong sense of time to exit it did.

This is true for entrepreneurs as well. Sometimes, they are so used to the incremental approach of business that they miss the big picture and don't realize the opportunity based on which they had built the business has either changed or ceased to exist. For technology businesses, if one makes a wrong bet on the timing and holds back the decision, then technology changes fast and the value of the business is eroded.

The annals of entrepreneurship sing paeans of founders who stayed independent, turn down big acquisition offers and built world-class businesses. All students of entrepreneurship know how Zuckerberg turning down early offers to buy Facebook, and Larry Page and Sergey Brin rejected billion dollar offers to buy Google. More recently, Slack and Snapchat are known to have turned down billions. Amazon wanted to acquire Netflix and upon its rebuttal created Amazon Prime. It is rumored that the Bansals had also refused an acquisition offer from Future Group in India to build out Flipkart. Getting out early with a payday isn't as glorified as defying the odds and building things yourself are.

Paradoxically, there is an ugly flip side to this 'staying independent' choice. Lots of entrepreneurs are scorned and derided when they reject large acquisition offers only to see their businesses decline or remain zombies. Yahoo!, Zynga and Groupon have all been scathed with criticism after they refused large acquisition offers only to falter their course later.

So, the founders are caught in the middle. If you take an exit, you are seen to bail out and not glorified but if you reject the same offer only to struggle in years ahead, you are called an overambitious, delusional fool. This is one of the many paradoxes that entrepreneurs must deal with in their journey. You have worked hard to move from having nothing to a stage where you have everything, but if you take a wrong decision, going back to zero is not difficult.

TO DO OR NOT TO

Even if you have no intention of exiting your business soon, it is important to think through your options and have a strategy in place. Exit consideration is personal to the entrepreneur. Some of the reasons which work on the heads of a sole founder taking an exit are:

1. **Choppy Markets:** Sometimes, it makes sense to cash out because of uncertainty about future market developments. Recently, Kishore Biyani sold his retail stores, warehousing and logistics business to Reliance Retail in a slump sale amounting to ₹24,317 crore. In interviews, Kishore Biyani said that the uncertainty due to COVID-19 prompted him to take this decision. Sometimes, changes in business regulations or government policies can adversely affect a business.

In another case, a competitor enters the market and threatens your business model. It may make sense for the entrepreneur to preemptively plan and exit the business, in such situations.

2. **Fails to Take off:** If an entrepreneur continues losing money after having tried a variety of approaches to stabilize the business, it may sometimes be best to call it quits. Quitting might be a wise decision if you are several years into your venture as then at least your team and clients find a home.

3. **Zeal for Adventure:** Many entrepreneurs are motivated by novelty, by exciting new fields, by striking out on your own and doing something different every day. For them, the routine nature of a 9-to-5 job is mundane.

. Such entrepreneurs also get restless and bored once their business reaches a point where the model is proven and its simply an operational challenge. After all, you started your business to do something exciting, not to create your own day job! Consider selling up and rediscovering your spark in a new field. One might even have a new business idea of your own, devised while your current corporation was growing.

4. **Exhaustion:** Starting up and running a business is tiresome. One is constantly been pulled to fire fight and think of solutions for a constantly changing business landscape, which leads to exhaustion. Add to this dealing with financial uncertainty, and deals falling through with investors or customers. The more innovative the business idea, the less likely the average person is going to relate to you; feelings of loneliness are not uncommon. These are conditions that take a long-term toll on mental health.

5. **Lifestyle Change:** Having reached a certain stage, you may feel that your business doesn't suit your present lifestyle anymore. There could be several reasons:

   - You want to enjoy the rest of your life as you may have reached a certain financial success.
   - You may prefer now to spend more time with your family instead of working 60-hour weeks.
   - Starting a new hobby or rediscovering an old one.

- As you start to slow down physically, it's understandable that you would want to sell your business to spend your energy on your family rather than work all the time.

Phanindra Sama was one of the first B2C exits in India. He had raised about $10 million of seed and VC money and exited Redbus after seven years, in 2013, for around $120 million to Ibibo Group, a part of the South African Naspers Group. While this was lauded at that time as a game-changing transaction in the Indian consumer internet market, many wondered if it was too early.

Says Phani of the exit, seven years on, 'A lot has changed from our time to now. During our time, it was not at all common for founders to take some money off the table by selling some of their equity. Founders were supposed to have their skin in the game. The founder salaries were also not very good. But now founders and ESOP holders can sell some of their equity during fundraise. This is very good because it increases one's appetite to take risk. ESOP holders also feel good because their equity becomes liquid.'

Phani also shares that founder earlier would not get market salary. 'If I had continued in a regular job, I would be able to make ten-fold and a point comes when you question the value of the illiquid shares. I could not sell my shares and did not have any savings. The only way in those days to make money was through an exit. When I compared myself to my other peers, they were in a much better position; they had a car, house and some savings too. On that if the venture doesn't work then I have nothing. In that context if someone comes to buy, you take that opportunity. Today, of course the market has changed. I see a lot of founders sell some of their shares and get liquidity. The salary is much better for founders also. Hence the world has changed from then to now and what I did was the right thing for the founders at that time.'

However, if the start-up goes through various rounds of funding, then there is a need for clear articulation of an exit plan. This allows external investors to make realistic calculations of the timeline and likely rate of return on their investment, increasing the chances of investment by an angel or VC. Secondly, deciding how you want to exit enables you to structure the business so that it optimizes your return in case of such an exit.

All equity investors, including angels, VCs and PE firms, are reliant on the successful business exit to see a return on their investment. This means that entrepreneurs are extremely unlikely to raise equity funding from external investors unless they cover exit strategy in their pitch and business plan.

Entrepreneurs should research and know by what means and how soon similar companies in similar markets have been able to exit. In the context of externally funded start-ups, most often this will be through acquisition by a larger firm and occasionally through an IPO.

It is important for the entrepreneur to bear in mind that a lot of divergence in opinion occurs between investors, the board and the entrepreneur. This is a time that emotions run high and often result in misunderstandings and a soured relationship.

Negotiating with a buyer is a challenge for founders during an exit. But negotiating with one's own side—he investors—can be just as difficult, if not more so. These disagreements typically arise when start-ups get an offer to sell and the founders and venture investors disagree about what to do. The offer can be 'life-changing' for founders. But for venture investors, particularly with big funds exits are not appealing. To explain why, we need to look at how traditional venture funds are structured.

INVESTOR ECONOMICS

VCs typically want a good venture fund to make three to five times their money. In other words, a fund with ₹1000 crore invested would have to return ₹3000–₹5000 crore from the fund's companies that are acquired, IPO, or are otherwise sold off in some form. A 4 times return would net about a 2.5 times distribution to the fund's limited partners after fees to the general partners. So, VCs depend on massive 'home run' exits.

As a result, smaller exits are not that attractive to most large VCs, particularly if they have made a large investment. Many would rather not sell, and instead they roll the dice and hope for a larger outcome.

VCs often look at return on their money at the portfolio level rather than the company. There is nothing wrong or untoward in this, it is the nature of the beast.

Therefore, for a founder to get all to align their interest is key. While many VCs don't like to talk about it, their immediate economic interests can diverge from their start-ups, particularly in smaller acquisitions. For founders, especially those who are first-time founders, their tolerance for risk is usually lower. VCs are in the business of managing risk on a portfolio basis. For founders, an exit can be a once-in-a-lifetime chance to change their life for their family. For investors, the same transactions may be immaterial.

For founders it can be difficult to disagree with an investor on a sale. In particular, first-time founders often feel indebted to investors for taking a chance on them. Of course, not all investors have the same interests. The larger a VC fund, and the more of their money they have invested in a company, the less likely they are to like a smaller exit. Smaller seed investors or micro-VC funds, which are proliferating, do not need billion-dollar exits to return their funds, so they are happier with smaller exits.

Despite the potential conflict of interest, most investors do tend to back the entrepreneur as they realize that it is the entrepreneurs' vision and capability to take things ahead that the buyer is really interested in. Many VCs have rights they can use to try to block an acquisition. But most rarely use them, particularly if a founder makes a good case for a deal as the best possible outcome for a company. VCs do not want to be known as 'not founder friendly,' even if they hate a deal and feel it is unfair. But they'll complain privately.

BUYER VIEW

For buyers, of course, it is complicated when sellers and investors aren't on the same page. The motivation for a buyer is to keep the founder and the management team happy, as they will come into the company; yet seasoned buyers also try to see what works for the investors.

In India, acqui-hire—where a buyer just wants the team but not the product or IP—is gaining traction. Here, a buyer could just hire a start-up team and not pay the investors anything. But most big buyers want to stay on good terms with investors as use the VC investors portfolio as their deal flow pipeline for future acquisitions as well.

During this stressful time, a founder realizes that he is alone. While there are bankers and lawyers who will work with the board, the investors and the board keep their priority foremost. It is at these times, an advisor who the entrepreneur trusts come in handy.

Rajat Mohanty, founder and CEO of Paladion Networks which was recently acquired by Atos, shares his experience of exit. According to Rajat, there were enough options that came his way, especially because of the domain his company was in, cyber security. 'The offer had to make sense for the employees and clients. Our reputation in the market was well established so exiting meant to give away the business to someone that is equally well-know. Atos ranked third in cyber security globally, and with us they climbed up to the second position. The employees get a better option and a bigger platform. Same goes for clients as they get an assurance that they are in a better situation,' explained Rajat.

THE EXIT

Like in every step of the entrepreneurial journey, the exit must be planned out well. First you must understand the motivations of the buyer. It is essential to get a feel for that so you can then position your exit strategy in these lines. The usual drivers for buyers are:

- Cost synergies
- Revenue enhancers
- Acquiring newer markets
- Acquiring newer IP which will enhance the core business
- Kill competition
- Acquiring a team with complementary/newer skillsets
- Acquiring to make the business future proof

The buyers typically want to know three things:

- Is the IP really yours?

- Is the team capable of scaling up and will they stay post the acquisition?
- Will your customers stick around?

In this context, sooner than later, one needs to engage lawyers and accountants to complete the due diligence checklist. Early-stage companies have a lot of lacunae in paperwork and back office and it is important to get the house ready prior a trade sale.

To maximize the sale value, you need to prime and work towards ensuring the following:

- Client list—ramp it up and ensure long term contracts
- Additional revenue streams—show newer revenue streams in recent months from same client set or newer clients making it particularly attractive to potential buyers.
- Team spirit—get the entire team especially, the core team, members to rally behind the strategy and ensure they are motivated for the trade sale.
- Product—launching product set as an excellent indicator of potential, new long-term growth and adds a very favourable aspect to the sale.
- Scalability—buyers like scalable business as they feel that by putting in more capital into the business, they can have still bigger returns.
- Market positioning and brand—if you want to sell your business and get the best ROI, then you have to demonstrate future growth and potential. No buyer is interested in past performance; regardless of how stunning it may have been. Business success is always about future rewards.

As you can see from the above, there are lots of reasons why 'now' could be the right time to sell your business. Like most aspects of business though, this too requires a strategy which takes a number of different factors into account. That's because the idea is to strike when the iron isn't just hot, but positively sizzling.

If you've done your homework properly you will know yourself when the best time to advertise your business for sale is. The next step is to convince the potential buyer that this is their golden opportunity for growth—both for the business and their own personal fortune.

THE IPO

Exits are what give liquidity to the entrepreneurs and the driver for the VC ecosystem. However, the holy grail for liquidity is not the IPO market. Globally, less than 5 per cent of VC invested companies go for an IPO. In India, the number is still less. There have been handful of companies that have been start-ups and have gone public.

For IPO businesses you need different skill sets as entrepreneurs and the thinking of the exit is very different. You provide liquidity for yourself and the investors but you are still running the business. One of the aberrations in this market is my friend Sudip Bandyopadhyay, the group chairman of Inditrade Capital. He not only started his entrepreneurial journey on the other side of the 40s but made his debut by acquiring a listed firm, that too after spending over two decades of his life into firms like Unilever, ITC, Reliance and New Silk Route.

When I asked him if handling a listed firm has its challenges, he said: 'I have worked with both listed and private firms, let me tell you there are advantages of a listed firm. One of the advantages is that it builds discipline within the organization. For instance, your accounting procedures have to be completed within a stipulated time, every quarter for publication of results, presence of independent directors etc. Second, the listed company gives me a flexibility to merge some of my other subsidiaries into it and give my investors an exit.'

I think what worked in Sudip's favour is his vast experience with large firms and the fact that he has seen all the formats of enterprises— promoter-driven, listed, PE-driven and a large conglomerate too.

One of the most talked about IPOs in the Indian start-up segment has been of Speciality Restaurant. 'We had built this organization carefully with a bigger picture in mind—of being a listed company one day. It's been my life's goal really,' explains Anjan Chatterjee, a hotel management graduate, and later, an advertising guy, who opened up his first restaurant

on the behest of friends who didn't want his cooking skills to go to waste.
But, from his first kitchen in Only Fish, Chatterjee knew he'd found his
calling—to build a restaurant company that was founded with sound
business fundamentals, yet gave foodies a great eating experience.

Chatterjee shares with me that the response for the IPO was way
beyond his expectations, 'I'll never forget the last day of the listing all my
life. We took two years to prepare ourselves for public issues. Unfortunately
as we approached the launching, the market turned pessimistic. But look at
the confidence of our dear investors, we had a fabulous opening,' he says.

In May 2012, SRL went public, raising ₹182 crore from the issue.
Despite the public issue being launched at a time when the markets were
particularly choppy, and against conventional wisdom, SRL generated
substantial investor enthusiasm and was oversubscribed 2.5 times and
nearly 4.7 times in the qualified institutional buyer (QIB) segment.

Of course, post-IPO, both the stakes and the responsibility have got
higher. 'It's a huge challenge, to make a promise and be able to keep it.
I feel honoured that so many investors have trusted us. We have to work
much harder. An IPO is not about accumulating public wealth. It's about
performance. It should be driven by need (to grow), not by greed.'

Anand Deshpande too shares similar emotions when I asked him
about his experience of the IPO. 'One of the reasons was to give exit
to investors. An IPO is a big landmark in a founder's life, not everyone
gets to see this. It is one of those experiences as an entrepreneur that
cannot be defined or explained. It's an exciting process and you have to
be fortunate to be able to do this,' says Anand.

Other than the presence of external investors who needed an exit,
many companies of their size or thereabout had come up with an IPO.
Anand also describes that the IPO was a milestone or was one of the
transition phases for the company. 'IPO also meant you are answering
analysts every quarter. People who are buying your shares are only
interested in short-term gains. They are looking at predictability. Lot
of times your share price depends on how the analysts estimate your
numbers than what you achieve, and you get bench marked with other
companies. There are good and bad aspects to this. Good is that it forces
you to be on the treadmill for some time. Bad is that it puts pressure on

the company,' says Anand.

But more importantly, IPO also becomes an exit for employees to value and sell their ESOPs. 'We had also done ESOPs in 1999–2000. After that we raised a small amount from Intel in 2001. It pegged a valuation for the first time, which also meant that people with ESOPs actually had shares which would be of value. So, unless you sell out or come with an IPO, you cannot get an exit for these ESOPs,' says Anand.

GETTING START-UP BATTLE READY

- Time your exits with milestones of the company.
- Taking advice from a mentor about dealing with existing investors on exit can be helpful.
- Exit or sell-off should be beneficial for all the stakeholders within the company.
- Decide at the very start what is it that you thrive for; sell off or an IPO.
- If going for an IPO, be prepared to answer the analyst and also keep up with the swinging of share prices.

17

ENTREPRENEURS DON'T FAIL, BUSINESSES DO

When I was talking to Saumil Majmudar, CEO and founder of SportzVillage, the first thing he shared with me was his experience with failure.

'Something that a lot of people do not talk about is that my first two ventures failed. My venture failing took a toll on me. I mean I had not experienced failure before. I was a good student; graduated from IIT Bombay, IIM Bangalore. But failing at the venture was an intense period and an event which our education system and our families do not prepare us for. After the dust settled, I realized that if I would have just hung in there, I would have made it,' said Saumil.

What also worked in Saumil's case to gather all the courage and again take the plunge as an entrepreneur, was his family support. 'After my venture failed, I was at a family wedding and everyone within the family knew about my failed business. One of my uncles came to me and said: "Your venture has failed, you are not a failure." I thought that was very important,' shares Saumil

True entrepreneurs never fail. They draw learnings from their failed businesses and come back stronger the next time around. Failure is inherent in start-ups and entrepreneurship. In fact, many entrepreneurs consider failure to be a natural stepping stone to success. They celebrate failure, because they've learned firsthand that mistakes are the greatest sources of learning.

In India, till recently, failure was a taboo. Given the hyper-competitive zeal to succeed and pressure from peers and family, we grew up in a culture where failures were looked down upon. People therefore, in India in the last century would not be risk-takers. They would flow with the tide and ensure a modicum of success. It bred a culture of mediocrity and lack of excellence and innovation. The educational system also didn't encourage any 'out-of-the-box' moves and forced a straight-jacketed view of life.

But in the last decade or so, things have changed drastically in India. The education system has started to encourage risk-taking and today in IIT Kharagpur, students can take academic breaks and try their hand at start-ups and if they fail can come back to complete their studies.

Failure has started to be accepted as the other side of the coin of success. There are a number of innovative and new business models that are being tried out and most of them accost failures. But the failures are not deterring the entrepreneurs to re-launch themselves with newer ideas. Investors like us are constantly looking to back failed entrepreneurs as we feel they have learned deep lessons and won't repeat their mistakes. Slowly but surely, within the entrepreneurial ecosystem, people are realizing that 'you can't keep a true and honest entrepreneur down'.

In Silicon Valley, failure has been treated as the warp and woof of an entrepreneur's life for a long time. The most successful entrepreneurs have had their early failures. In his first letter to shareholders in 1997, Jeff Bezos, founder and CEO of Amazon wrote, 'We will continue to learn from both our successes and our failures.' Since then, almost every letter to Amazon's shareholders has contained the words 'invent' and 'fail'—continually emphasizing how tolerance for failure is a large part of Amazon's culture and success.

Similarly, in the 2016 shareholder letter, Bezos wrote, 'One area where I think we are especially distinctive is failure. I believe we are the best place in the world to fail (we have plenty of practice!).' He has further said, 'Given a 10 per cent chance of a 100 times payoff, you should take that bet every time. But you're still going to be wrong nine times out of 10.'

Entrepreneurship, especially innovation-focused entrepreneurship, is very much like a science—involving a series of experiments that can bring something new and valuable into the world. You cannot learn what product or idea will work without being willing to discover what won't work. This is known by every successful entrepreneur, most of whom have business 'failures' in their portfolios. Before Evan Williams started Twitter, he founded Odeo, the podcasting platform you've never heard of. Before Reid Hoffman created LinkedIn, he launched SocialNet, a dating site that didn't connect. Nick Woodman shuttered EmpowerAll.com and Funbug before clicking with GoPro.

FAILING TO SUCCEED

Hindsight is 20:20. There can be as many reasons for entrepreneurs to fail as there are reasons to succeed. Sometimes the writing is on the wall but many fail to see it, in some case the decision taken regarding partners or inability to raise funds or even the mercurial temperament can take the better off a start-up.

Steve Andriole, the Thomas G. Labrecque, professor of Business Technology in the Villanova University, in an article for Forbes[16] describes 10 reasons why entrepreneurs fail, and I strongly agree with him. Following are the 10 reasons:

1. Not Smart Enough
    Not talking about IQ here. Entrepreneurial IQ (EIQ) is about a holistic understanding of situations. Many entrepreneurs understand their own idea, but not the market that will accept or reject it. Nor do they understand how accidental, uncontrollable, unscheduled innovation actually works. Or who the real competitors are. Often, entrepreneurs have too little domain depth: they do not know what they're talking about (though they often talk a good game). Many entrepreneurs fail because they're not truly entrepreneurs but some variation on the theme. Even worse are entrepreneurs who believe they're terrific at activities, while everyone around them think they're horrible at it. If an entrepreneur is incapable of seeing what everyone else sees, he or she is blind to success.

---

[16]'10 Reasons Why Entrepreneurs Fail.' *Forbes*. www.forbes.com/sites/steveandriole/2016/04/01/10-reasons-why-entrepreneurs-fail/#28ba751f42d9. Accessed 21 November 2020.

2. Not Knowing Who's Who

   When you are on your own and going against the tide by creating a new business, you are always looking for people who will encourage you. But knowing the difference between genuine encouragement and 'yes men' who have no idea where you are heading, is important. In Chapter 9, there is mention of how one needs to be careful about investors who may go over the moon to court you, but ultimately will not put any money in the bank. Entrepreneurs often fail because they cannot separate friends from enemies. They fail because they cannot separate inconsistent angel investors from disciplined ones. I always ask entrepreneurs to do reference check on the investors who they plan to onboard.

3. Not Finding Enough (of the Right Kind of) Funding

   Successful entrepreneurs are those who follow the balance sheet and always work towards generating enough cash, and those who have their ears to the ground and are realists when it comes to valuations. Entrepreneurs often fail because they cannot raise the right kind of funding at the right time and at the right valuation. They fail to appreciate how much money it takes to meet milestones. Inexperienced founders confuse the act of raising capital with achieving the business plan.

4. Grandiose Expectations

   Every entrepreneur believes that their idea/product will revolutionize the market. One has to realize that coming up with an idea is just the first step, execution and taking the idea to reality is a different game. Entrepreneurs who fail, often do so because they believe they will change the world and if the world doesn't welcome their authority, it's the world's fault, not theirs.

5. Horrible Soft Skills

   Entrepreneurs often need to be outspoken and many a times need to call a spade a spade. The other trait that makes for a successful entrepreneur is the art of listening. If you are one of those who is intolerant of other views, then failing is a possibility to be prepared for. This is also true for those who have a successful corporate career before they start their entrepreneurial journey. Taking responsibility of mistakes and moving on should always be your game.

6.　Bad Partners

Partners here refers to people whom you interact with on a daily basis for guidance, advice and mentoring. If having a bad co-founder results in a weak foundation for your dream business, then colleagues and mentors who cannot give you the right advise are equally harmful for you and your start-up. Good entrepreneurs have a purpose-filter through which they pass their time: *is this partner really worth my time?* Entrepreneurs who fail do not have this filter.

7.　Ineffective Sales

As mentioned in Chapter 7, an entrepreneur has to be the sales guy for his company. If you cannot get the right clients at the right time and for the right price, then do not expect your sales team to do wonders.

8.　Market Invisibility

Spending big bucks in the initial stages of growth to make your presence felt may be expensive, but that does not mean there are no smarter means of reaching to your customer or letting the markets know about your presence. Smart entrepreneurs often successfully leverage their alma matter for spreading the word. Using all available media, especially digital media should be your focus: *if they cannot find you, they cannot buy you.*

9.　Pivot Paralysis

Entrepreneurship is all about remaining focused on your goals, yet at the same time having the ability to change the course of your blueprint. Most of the time businesses fail because they cannot adapt to a sudden shift in events and conditions. All start-ups require pivots. Unsuccessful entrepreneurs cannot pivot.

10.　No Sense of the Inevitable Exit

As much as you might like to be at the helm of your business, it is wise to also be mentally prepared to exit the business. You may find it difficult to detach yourself from your start-up as you have nurtured it as your own. Is the exit an IPO or an acquisition? Is it an acqui-hire or a recapitalization? Good entrepreneurs have a sense of how an exit will occur (if one occurs at all), within a year of their launch. Bad ones believe in miracles.

GET UP AGAIN

Every failure has a lesson that needs to be understood by the entrepreneur and the society at large. True entrepreneurs work to use their failures to their future advantages. Smart entrepreneurs often turn their lemons into lemonade when failure comes knocking.

BE HONEST WITH YOURSELF

When failure comes, and the entrepreneur finds out that they have fallen short of their own expectations, they need to acknowledge it. They don't need to be in a state of denial or shy away from it. They need to tell the same to all stakeholders, be it the staff, the clients, the bankers, etc. They need to disclose the same to their family and friends and other well-wishers. If family and friends find out about it themselves, then it would be a double failure. They might even begin to wonder why the entrepreneur kept it secret and might dismiss it as cowardice.

EXPLAIN WHAT HAPPENED BUT NEVER MAKE EXCUSES

When something goes wrong, people are less likely to take responsibility for it. They shy away from it and make piles of excuses for their failure. Running away from responsibility will never help the entrepreneur grow. You must first admit your mistakes before your mind can be in the space it needs to be to think of remedies to the situation. There may be others who are at greater fault, but the buck always stops with the founder.

LET YOUR ANGER OVER THE FAILURE DRIVE YOU

True entrepreneurs have a positive ego. They treat this failure as a stepping stone. The anger passions their motivation to succeed next time around.

EMBRACE FAILURE AS A SIDE EFFECT OF INNOVATION

Sometimes, failure is a function of time. An entrepreneur may have a bright idea, even executed it well but the market was not ready for the same. This is not a sign of your failure. That is why investors back multi-entrepreneurs as they are innovative and look at future trends.

NO GUTS, NO GLORY

Take the case of Abhishek Negi. He comes from an army background and studied electrical engineering from IIT Kharagpur and graduated in 2013. He joined Vodafone as product manager but quit in 2014 and started Roder, earlier known as InstaCab. This was the first investment Unicorn India Ventures had made from its first fund. But the business had to wind off as competition from well-entrenched players like Ola and Uber had made it difficult to continue.

According to Abhishek, 'It takes a toll both mentally and physically. Roder was one of the biggest failures of my life. I put a lot of expectations on it. We tried a lot to save the business. Then came a stage where we were trying to salvage something to give back to the investors, but over time we realized that shutting down was the only option,' he shared.

He does advise budding entrepreneurs that, 'You may have lost and the dream that you were working towards will not see the light of the day, but it is better to make peace with it and move on. Everything matters; friends, co-founder, investors, and you all are in the same ship. Your family suffers too. You have fought with them and convinced them hard that this is what you want to do and how that job is not good enough and now you go back to them when you fail. Dealing with family is still ok. But to put behind investors backing and the third-party dealing that you have are difficult to manage. But I have learnt a lesson. We are humans and we will make mistakes, perhaps the same ones too. But I think if I can avoid even 50 per cent of the mistakes that I made then I would have broken some ground.'

After the failure, Abhishek went into a shell and didn't know how to accost failure. 'I had till then always got what I wanted. I did a lot of soul searching. I did get a very good offer from other big companies in this space. It was really hard to reject that but I thought '*Ek baar aur fight marni hai*' (I will try once more). A human lives for 70–80 years and it's just one life that you get, and if you have support, in my case my family, and guts as well; why not do it again,' he said.

Abhinay Choudhari is another seasoned entrepreneur who learned from the failures of his first business. After his IIM Ahmedabad days, Abhinay used to work with Mitsubishi and in 1999 in the first wave of the dotcom, started a business called Style Country in the area of fashion ecommerce. He raised money and carried the business for couple of years. He soon realized that the company couldn't scale as the net penetration in India was abysmally low and also, with the internet crash of 2000, funding was starved. He went ahead and had a successful corporate career and then started ShopasUlike in 2008. This was the basis of the creation of BigBasket in 2011, and as they say, the rest is history.

It is said, failure forms the foundation for success. Nowhere is it truer than the start-up world. Founders need to remember this and come out of their venture failures unscathed mentally.

GETTING START-UP BATTLE READY

- Don't be disheartened by failures. They form the basis for future success.
- Sometimes failures happen through no fault of yours; circumstances and market conditions lead to failures.
- Don't flog a dead horse. Sometimes, it is better to recognize failure in a venture and move on.
- Don't make excuses for failure and inform all stake holders about the same.
- Society must accept failures for innovation and entrepreneurship to grow.
- Even in shutting down, you can come across as honourable with your employees, your investors and other stake holders.

18

DEFINING THE SECOND INNINGS: NEWER PASTURES, NEWER CHALLENGES

Phanindra Sama, after his exit of Redbus, didn't start another venture. Instead, he worked with the Government of Telangana to nurture the start-up ecosystem there, for over five years. Says Phani 'When I exited Redbus, I was 32, and if at that time I would have started another company, I would have had to give it at least 15 years. The other option was to spend time with family, which I had not been able to do, travel and also upgrade my knowledge/skills for five years and then start-up again. While on break, I was approached by the Government of Telangana to be the chief innovation officer, and I took up that role because I wanted to give back to society.'

Exit represents a high point for anyone who achieves it, but it also marks a step into the unknown for many entrepreneurs. From an outsider's perspective, there are few who wouldn't want what life after a business exit seems to offer the entrepreneur. One day you are doing what you have done for years, working hard and focusing on keeping the business on track; the next day, you wake up and the financial reward of all your effort is sitting in a bank account. You have the wealth, time and freedom to do whatever you choose. For every entrepreneur who experiences this moment, they quickly realize it will define the next stage of their life as much as the original act of starting the business.

But while much is written about the trials and tribulations of entrepreneurs as they grow their businesses, little attention is given to how entrepreneurs live through this next phase of their entrepreneurial career—if indeed 'career' is the right word. The fact is that, for all but the most high-profile entrepreneurs, the business exit happens under the radar of publicity. As a trade buyer or management team quietly takes over, the entrepreneur slips away into the shadows to walk a new path. So, what exactly does happen next? Where do these entrepreneurs go? And what do they do? It is interesting to explore how entrepreneurs manage to balance the opportunity which a successful business exit presents, with the challenge of reinventing a new life.

ADJUSTMENT TO THE NEW NORMAL IS NOT EASY

Building a fulfilling lifestyle post-exit is harder than many entrepreneurs anticipate. When it comes to life after exit, entrepreneurs have high expectations about what that life will bring. The vast majority expect a lifestyle which is at least as fulfilling as the one they had running their own business and, for the most part, life post-exit delivers on that expectation. But although nearly all entrepreneurs end up satisfied with their life post-exit, many underestimate the challenge of arriving at that point of satisfaction. Something that takes entrepreneurs by surprise in their post-exit careers, is that the process of reinvention will not necessarily be as easy as many expect.

An entrepreneur will not know what to do after they sell, so seeking advice from those who have done it already will make the transition smoother. Planning may not help entrepreneurs adapt to a new life after they exit their business, but one area which will pay dividends is to understand the common areas which either aid or obstruct the process of reinvention.

Entrepreneurs often suffer from 'seller's remorse'. They often feel that the deal wasn't good enough. They feel that they miss the action and the adrenaline flow that goes with creating a business. They often hear stories about the newer buyers changing personnel and strategy that were so dear to them and they feel that things aren't going in the right direction. This gives them a sense of remorse and wanting to go back.

The real benefit of life after exit is freedom of choice. Because both time and money are finite, it is important to be clear about the activities which you want to get involved in as it is easy to get sucked into ones which you don't want to do. Don't assume everything you do will be a success.

This is the lifestyle choices of entrepreneurs post-exit: few are prepared to walk away from being involved in a business. Rather than reinvent themselves as an investor or adviser, when it comes to life post-exit, the first choice for the majority of entrepreneurs is to do it all again. Entrepreneurs thrive on the excitement and specificity of envisioning the future and planning for it.

THE DO'S OF POST-EXIT LIFE

1. Make clean legal breaks with clear contracts. This is key as you don't want to be mired with legal hassles after the exit. Having a lawyer alongside you in the whole journey is very important.
2. Give yourself the same attention you would a promising new venture. Don't be in a rush to get involved with something to keep the networks alive. This is a cardinal mistake most exited entrepreneurs make, including myself. You get into business that you do not understand and then you undergo the associated pain.
3. Downsize your options before you choose. Don't be in a hurry to invest in angel investments, as you would be inundated with opportunities. Again, a mistake I made post my exits and something which is common to most entrepreneurs.
4. Surround yourself with people who inspire new growth. While you have been building your business, the business world has changed. You do become dated in the larger context. It is important to make oneself contemporary once again with newest trends and technology. A lot of entrepreneurs even go back to school.

STARTING THE ENTREPRENEURSHIP JOURNEY AGAIN

Within our portfolio companies, we have a few second-time entrepreneurs. We can clearly see the approach, which is different from the first-time entrepreneurs. This is irrespective of whether the first venture was a failure or a success—there are learnings in both the cases. Here are some of the things that an experienced entrepreneur and angle investor Feliks Eyser shared in an article for *Medium*[17] comparing first-time and second-time entrepreneurs.

Some of the things that the second-time entrepreneurs avoid is micro management. They prefer to either hire a team that has experience in handling specific operations or those who have had experience with the situations that arise in start-ups beforehand. Serial entrepreneurs are also financially wise. They have already witnessed how access to funds can make or break the road-map of a start-up. This means they may either raise fewer large funds or focus on their shareholding.

Most of the time, you will hear first-time founders complain that they hardly get time to focus on business strategy as they are busy courting investors or raising funds. Second-timers have gone through this cycle and hence, now look for the right investors and high valuation.

Entrepreneurs should remember that while they are creating a business and bringing out new products or services into the market, you will need employees to run the ship. Hence, hiring the right people is a must. Second-time founders are aware of this and their priority is to hire the right people when in growth mode. They know the cost of a bad hire.

Another aspect that second-timers get right is customer engagement. They know that if they want their product to be truly outstanding, then customer insight and feedback is crucial.

Serial entrepreneurs and some founders who have had a successful corporate career know the importance of processes. Many start-up founders, especially the first-timers, believe that processes are unnecessary shackles of corporate world. Processes, however, bring in clarity that helps in scaling.

In short, the learnings from the first venture, success or failure, remains

---

[17]"What Successful Second-Time Founders Do Differently." *Medium.* https://marker.medium.com/what-successful-second-time-founders-do-differently-2f368ae2e31f. Accessed 21 November 2020.

with the entrepreneur and the second-time around they achieve a better parenting role with their child than they did with the first.

◆

Whatever may be your decision, sell-off or giving away your active role in the company and being on the board as an advisor, own it and embrace it. There will always be pressure to start a new venture, and there will be enough opportunities to become an investor, or you may want to part your knowledge with new budding entrepreneurs, but before doing anything just take a long breath and relax.

Afterword

TRANSFORMING INDIA THROUGH AN
ENTREPRENEURIAL MINDSET

Entrepreneurship is a state of existence. While we understand it mostly in a business context, it is also a pillar of society and politics. It is this entrepreneurial mindset, which I feel will transform India in the decades to come.

In 1915, at the age of 45, an NRI lawyer named Mohandas Karamchand Gandhi returned to India. Over the next 33 years, he would give up his suit (symbolizing his legal career) for a short dhoti (exemplifying the requirements of his entrepreneurial journey), and transform himself, India's freedom struggle and Indian politics forever. He would inspire and impact millions around the world. How did he become the leader of millions of Indians? What enabled him to do this? It was the extraordinary combination of entrepreneurial traits that made Gandhi perhaps the first truly globally impactful 'political entrepreneur' in the best possible sense.

The traits were of deep reflection, self-awareness, an understanding of the context of the world around him and being able to confront and overcome his weaknesses.

For example, Gandhi attended a public speaking practice group in London to overcome his shyness and inhibition that would have impeded his law practice. He struggled till he found ways to deal with and overcome serious problems that he personally experienced and witnessed, constantly developing, reflecting, learning, evolving, expressing and acting out a personal manifesto of beliefs and ideas. He had the courage of his convictions to challenge the status quo and was unafraid to go against the most powerful Empire the world had ever known, while honing the skills of persuasion, mobilizing and organizing people around shared aspirations and a world view. He possessed incredible strength of mind, one that was almost impossible to change once made up, acting in a profoundly impactful way when opportunities presented themselves—the non-violence and non-cooperation movements, in Champaran or Kheda or the famous Dandi march.

Developing 'brand concepts' that resonated with people—swaraj, satyagraha, ahimsa and swadeshi—in order to galvanize people against the British was unparalleled or what we would call today as 'innovative and disruptive'. 'Walking the talk' while living his life in the public gaze created the Mahatma. So much so that Subhas Chandra Bose, who vehemently disagreed with Gandhi, was moved by respect and regard to refer to him as the Father of the Nation.

Gandhi was an incredible individual. Yet, these traits and behaviours exhibited by him are found, in varying degrees, in all of us. And most visibly seen in those with an entrepreneurial mind. Those that overcome seemingly intractable problems against all odds. Such individuals think in terms of possibilities, not constraints. They understand the power of imagination, willpower and perseverance. Their dogged pursuit of their vision attracts followers to their idea and inspires them to act in consonance and create a movement.

The same entrepreneurial traits were exhibited by Verghese Kurien, who transformed India from a milk-deficient country to the world's largest producer of milk with 21 per cent of the global milk production. In August 2020, Amul, the Gujarat Cooperative Milk Marketing Federation (GCMMF), with a turnover of US$5.5 billion, became the first Indian dairy company to feature in the Dutch multinational and financial services company Rabobank's Global Top 20 list. It was a breathtaking achievement for the 3.6 million-strong milk producers' cooperative.

Just like entrepreneurs have mentors, Gandhi had a Gopal Krishna Gokhale, and Kurien had a Tribhuvandas Patel, who in 1949 persuaded Kurien to set up a dairy cooperative. The dairy cooperative model focused on the economic self-interest of farmers outside of entrenched vested interests. Kurien consolidated farmers and eliminated middlemen. He lobbied against imports of butter and condensed milk which he realized were being used by countries to convert their aid to trade for their own benefit; he used dumped aid from Europe during a period of enormous glut in production there to launch his 'billion litre idea' and Operation Flood, where high-yield native cattle were moved to urban areas along with the setting up of milk sheds and dairy farms across the country.

A newly independent, poor, infrastructure- and resource-starved country used the expertise, technology, research and aid from foreign countries to its advantage under Kurien's visionary leadership, to make skimmed milk powder, condensed milk and even cheese from buffalo milk which was more abundant than cow milk in India, unlike in Europe. He had been earlier told that such products from buffalo milk 'could not be left to the natives'. From keeping politicians and bureaucrats from meddling in dairy cooperatives, establishing the GCMMF that brought together all dairy cooperatives under a single roof, establishing the now iconic Amul brand, setting up the National Dairy Development Board, facilitating the setting up of state milk federations, to even establishing the Institute for Rural Management to groom managers for the cooperatives, the 'Father of the White Revolution' made dairy farming India's largest self-sustaining industry and the largest rural employment sector, providing a third of all rural income.

Kurien, like Gandhi, has been accused of being obstinate, relentless and ruthlessly focused on achieving his goals. Again, traits shared by successful entrepreneurs. They work with people of all kinds, bring them together in order to achieve a goal. One that is missionary and aspirational. After all, what is the point of being an entrepreneur and doing something that isn't?

Entrepreneurs become great when they are encouraged to think of 'Big Hairy Audacious Goals', of having a purpose that transcends the immediate, of attacking large problems, of leading and motivating teams. Management gurus have long exhorted that the best way to predict the future is to invent it. And one can only invent the future if we can all collectively imagine one.

It was one such imagined future of a corruption-free India that led to the India Against Corruption (IAC) movement in 2011. Rocked by tales of unbridled and pervasive political corruption, non-violent protests and demonstrations broke out across the country when anti-corruption activist and Gandhian Anna Hazare began a hunger strike to demand the passing of a Jan Lokpal Bill. Social media helped spread the word and helped mobilize a Dandi March II, as Indians across the country united in their demand for a new India. Fazed by this, the government agreed to set up a Lokpal Bill under the Chairmanship of the veteran politician, the late Pranab Mukherjee who went on to become the President of India.

One of the members of this drafting committee was then a little-known RTI activist named Arvind Kejriwal, an alum from IIT Kharagpur. After a series of meetings, drafts, parliamentary debates, protests, hunger strikes, speeches, rallies, tumultuous scenes in public, drama and more, the Lokpal Bill failed to be passed in Parliament. Members of the Anna Hazare team were divided on how to take forward the movement they had unwittingly seeded. Arvind Kejriwal, as one of the key campaigners of the IAC, saw the future lay in political mobilization around the sentiments aroused by the IAC movement.

Like a true entrepreneur, he seized the moment offered by Anna Hazare. He formed the Aam Aadmi Party (AAP) on 26 November 2012, contested the 2013 Delhi legislative assembly elections and emerged as the second largest political party. Today, AAP with a jhadoo or broom as its symbol, is a significant force in Delhi. Over the last eight years, it has matured from a political start-up to becoming nationally known, from being theatrical, immature and melodramatic to becoming seasoned and sober, from biting off more than it could chew to remaining focused on Delhi politics. It learnt how to effectively take on the opposition, understood the value of perception and media management and remained focused on its core constituency, namely the urban middle and lower middle classes. It now understands that education and healthcare are important for its core support base and has built a successful governance narrative around these. This is a most remarkable achievement for such a young party. Arvind Kejriwal saw the opportunity, understood the mood of the urban classes and grabbed the opportunity to successfully parlay his crusade against corruption into a political party, attracted funds and talent, and has since become a nationally known figure.

To be sure, Arvind Kejriwal used all the tools available to launch and then make AAP: from his style of dressing to making frequent social media-savvy statements, pitting himself and AAP against far better known and resourced rivals. AAP as a political start-up positioned itself as the 'David' against the Goliaths and launched itself brilliantly but then, like all other start-ups that need to grow beyond the press attention at launch, has stumbled, with many members of the core team quitting, its biting off more than it could chew as it attempted to expand outside Delhi, and its attempts to build a dominant narrative beyond its initial anti-corruption sloganeering. It is critical that, like start-ups that need to outgrow their early years to become a stable growing national player, AAP too needs to think afresh about its proposition, its target audience, attract talent, resources and most importantly execute relentlessly. The parallels from the worlds of start-ups and entrepreneurship are obvious.

Such entrepreneurial mindsets can also be used to profoundly alter the cultural and creative economy of India. Especially with global trends favouring sustainable, experiential lifestyles. For example, why shouldn't Indian companies and India be leading players in say, the global health and wellness industries? After all, yoga is an $80 billion business worldwide while the worldwide wellness industry is an estimated $4.7 trillion. The world food services business is worth an estimated $3 trillion, while the Indian food services market size was estimated at just $56 billion in 2018–19. With a massive range of cooking styles, a vast array of recipes from all states of India, heady aromatic flavours, bewildering spread of ingredients and immense health benefits, Indian cuisine can be a global foodie's choice from fine dining to street food.

Our epics offer a treasure trove of material for hugely successful media and entertainment franchises to be built. Why should Marvel, Harry Potter, Lord of the Rings or Game of Thrones, for example, have the monopoly? We need to think differently, of possibilities, of creating organized cultural ecosystems that challenge and change passive status quoist approaches. Why cannot Indian start-ups and entrepreneurs emerge as nationally and globally successful brands?

It is however important to also wake up to the fact that India is 102nd on the Global Hunger Index 2019 with alarming hunger levels across India. That, even after lifting 270 million people out of extreme poverty while doubling per capita GDP between 2005 to 2016, India still has 73 million people living in extreme poverty and 370 million people who do not get three meals a day. To alleviate the hunger of school children, the Akshaya Patra Foundation was set up in 2000. Its mission: 'No child in India shall be deprived of education because of hunger' attracted top talent from all over. It is run with a combination of entrepreneurial zeal and corporate sector rigour, discipline, systems and processes. It partners with governments, foundations, corporations, individuals and others today to provide meals to over 1.8 million children each day from state-of-the-art kitchens. A great lesson in using the entrepreneurial mindset in furthering its vision.

With about 25 million births a year and 9 million graduates a year, India needs to be able to provide jobs for these vast numbers, providing healthcare, nourishment, housing, education and a decent standard of living. Strategic areas of the economy like defense and telecom are almost entirely dependent on imports, making India vulnerable to external pulls and pushes.

The 21st century is going to be about countries leveraging their knowledge capital to stake their places in the rapidly emerging new world order. Innovative thinking, data-based decision-making, technology, ease of doing business and ease of living will be the leitmotifs of this era. This humongous task cannot just be outsourced to the government. It is up to all of us to think entrepreneurially, to challenge the passive status quo, change the dominant narratives in our politics, governance, society, economics, companies and culture, to make a difference, to create wealth, and to put India on a trajectory that it deserves to be on. The good news is that changes are afoot in all of the above. We cannot take comfort in a satisficing approach that keeps us as hapless spectators in this journey of change; it is time to become participants by becoming entrepreneurially minded in an ethical way. We need to learn from, and then act, in our own ways, on the extraordinary stories of the entrepreneurially minded. Only then can this transformation occur.

In 2016, the word 'start-up' entered the lexicon of the Government of India. It is time that the entrepreneurial mindset of a start-up enters and thrives within the Government in as much as it thrives without!

Can each one of us reading these pages pledge to create or enable the creation of at least 100 jobs in each of our lifetimes? This will require us to have the great entrepreneur's sense of mission.

As the Brihadaranyaka Upanishads IV.4.5 says:

You are what your deep driving desire is.
As your desire is, so is your will.
As your will is, so is your deed.
As your deed is, so is your destiny.

Do we have the deep driving desire of the entrepreneurial mind to transform India?

Sanjay Anandaram
3 September 2020

INDEX